**Introduction to
e Humanities**

The Open University

Religion and
Science in Context

Block

4

This publication forms part of an Open University course A(ZX)103 *An Introduction to the Humanities*. Details of this and other Open University courses can be obtained from the Student Registration and Enquiry Service, The Open University, PO Box 197, Milton Keynes, MK7 6BJ, United Kingdom: tel.+44 (0)870 333 4340, email general-enquiries@open.ac.uk

Alternatively, you may visit the Open University website at http://www.open.ac.uk where you can learn more about the wide range of courses and packs offered at all levels by The Open University

To purchase a selection of Open University course materials visit http://www.open.ac.uk, or contact Open University Worldwide, Michael Young Building, Walton Hall, Milton Keynes MK7 6AA, United Kingdom for a brochure. tel. +44 (0)1908 858785; fax +44 (0)1908 858787; e-mail ouwenq@open.ac.uk

The Open University
Walton Hall, Milton Keynes
MK7 6AA

First published 1998. Second edition 2001. Third edition 2003. Fourth edition 2005.

Edited and designed by The Open University.

Typeset by The Open University.

Printed and bound in Malta by Gutenberg Press.

ISBN 0 7492 9668 2

4.1

31612B/a103b4i4.1

INTRODUCTION TO BLOCK 4

Written for the course team by Gwilym Beckerlegge

Block 4 introduces the remaining Humanities disciplines, Religious Studies and History of Science. It builds on skills you have developed in previous blocks, particularly those of critical, close reading and historical argument.

Religious Studies and the History of Science: it would hardly be surprising if you immediately assumed that this block would be devoted to the great debates, some would say conflicts, between religion and science. But why should that be so? The growth of scientific inquiry in the nineteenth century and, in particular, the popularization of the theory of evolution did provoke considerable heart-searching on the part of many Victorian Christians as they felt compelled to reconsider their understanding of the world and humanity's place within it. You will find the periodicals of the day littered with signs of this confrontation between traditional religious convictions and new scientific thinking. Many of the great novels of the period also reflect this change in belief and some of the resulting tensions. In fact, you could trace the beginnings of this change back to the growth of rationalism during the period of the Enlightenment, touched on in Block 3, and the critical attitude this fostered towards the acceptance of religious teaching and authority. It is, perhaps, hardly surprising that those raised in this European intellectual tradition tend immediately to see religion and science in terms of conflict.

In fact, Block 4 does not revisit battlegrounds fought over by the respective defenders of religion and science. One reason for avoiding this important yet rather predictable focus is that not all religious traditions have undergone the same degree of discomfort in coming to terms with changes in scientific thinking as have some strands within Christianity. As you will shortly discover, this block makes reference to many religious traditions. Above all, this block is not designed to introduce you in great detail to forms of religion and science but to the *study* of religion (Religious Studies) and the History of Science. Now, you might immediately question whether it is possible to study anything without some understanding of what is to be studied. This block, of course, will be talking directly about science and religion. Its main concern, however, will be to outline the broad principles that govern the study of these two areas, rather than to explain particular scientific discoveries or introduce specific religious traditions at length. We shall leave that to second and third level courses.

So, why *have* the study of religion and the History of Science been put together in the same block? It is because both disciplines have to face certain problems in common. You will find that some of these problems appear little different from issues raised in earlier blocks; for example, looking for evidence and 'reading' it in a manner appropriate to the subject. Other general issues surface here in an acute form; for example, the debate about objectivity in the study of the Humanities. One problem, however, you will be meeting for the first time: what qualifies somebody to undertake the study of a subject? Let's begin by thinking about Block 4 in relationship to the earlier blocks in A103.

If you think back over your progress through A103 to date, you should be able to see that the course has been structured in such a way as to do more than simply introduce in turn different disciplines within the Humanities, together with their methods. Block 1 was primarily concerned to give you practice in skills of close looking, reading, listening and reasoning – skills that to some extent and to different degrees are common to the range of disciplines covered in A103. Nevertheless, in beginning to consider 'form' and 'meaning' you were also led to reflect even at the outset of the course on the way in which scholarly debate involves attempting to establish what we might term the 'boundaries' of what is being studied. In Block 4 we shall see that unresolved debates about both the definition of 'religion' and 'science' and the claims made by their practitioners have provoked discussion about the methods of Religious Studies and the History of Science and the boundaries of their respective fields of study.

You will find that emphasis upon the careful scrutiny of evidence and discussion of the boundaries of religion and science are central respectively to the study of religion and the History of Science (Units 14 and 15, Sections 2 and 3; Units 16 and 17, Section 5 and 6). Block 1, however, did not attempt to pursue questions about the context – historical, social and cultural – within which the artistic creations and the ideas considered in the block were both produced and studied. This kind of questioning provided a major part of the agenda for Blocks 2 and 3.

In Blocks 2 and 3 you met classicists and historians working to reconstruct not just the past but also sometimes the long-distant past of different countries and civilizations. Block 3 showed how bringing disciplines together can enrich our understanding of a certain period or set of problems. In both these blocks you began to use and evaluate historical sources, but you also had to wrestle with the problem of how students should respond to values, practices and assumptions very different from those they might hold personally. In exploring these kinds of questions, you also saw that scholars may well disagree about such matters, as they do over the causes of the French Revolution. The question of what students and scholars should do with their personal feelings is raised particularly sharply in the study of religion and the History of Science.

So what about Block 4? How does it fit into the underlying structure of A103? Well, first, as with the preceding blocks, it introduces new disciplines – Religious Studies and History of Science, the two remaining disciplines to be covered in the course. Block 4 brings these two disciplines together, however, in a way that you might not be expecting, having just completed an integrated study of the French Revolution. Block 4 introduces Religious Studies and History of Science by treating them in turn as illustrations of responses to common problems in these disciplines. As I have suggested, several of these problems are extensions of issues you have already met in the course:

- drawing 'boundaries'

- determining the 'form' of what is to be studied

- putting in context

- handling beliefs, values and practices that the individual student may be inclined to judge.

As we shall see, these problems, and especially the last point, are particularly prominent in Religious Studies and the History of Science because of the nature of their subject matter. In considering this last point, however, we shall also have to face more directly than in earlier parts of the course the question of whether initiation into the practice of certain disciplines in the Humanities is dependent upon some existing personal experience, skill or body of knowledge acquired by the student.

Now the last question might already have occurred to you as you worked your way from discipline to discipline. You might have wondered, for example, whether your insights into Art History and Music might have been more profound had you some talent as a practitioner – as an artist or musician. Similarly, you might have asked yourself whether the best literary critics are those who are also poets or novelists. These questions were not raised explicitly in the units and, of course, no suggestion was made that you had to be suitably 'qualified' in any of these ways to get the most from your encounter with these disciplines. The reason for this is that academic or scholarly study is distinct from the practice of the arts, although it is true that some scholars have been practitioners within the fields that they study. It is not generally assumed, however, that this kind of participation stands as some kind of entry requirement into these disciplines.

Let's now consider this from a different angle, but still thinking about personal qualities that a student might be asked to bring to a study. The issue of personal participation and speaking from this experience clearly does not surface in the study of the remote past, although it might do in the historical study of recent periods like the 1960s. Yet here too, whether in the study of the Colosseum or the French Revolution, something other than the application of an academic technique was asked of you; namely, the willingness to engage in the pursuit of an objective study – putting on hold your own assumptions and values in order to understand other people, another time, on their own terms. During your work on Philosophy, the insistence that you test rationally the validity of arguments, rather than leaping onto your own soapbox, might have come hard when thinking about issues like boxing or human rights. It would seem that practising an academic discipline involves a degree of self-discipline and standing back to allow the evidence to speak clearly for itself. After all, it is not simply the absorption of knowledge that distinguishes a scholarly discussion from a popular discussion of a controversial work of art or ethical issue, but a willingness to lay one's own prejudices aside in order to gain clarity of understanding.

In Block 4, you will be asked to consider two disciplines in which there have been fundamental debates about the 'qualifications' required by anybody wishing to become involved respectively in the study of religion and the History of Science. Units 14 and 15, Section 6, outlines what has been a profoundly influential, but fiercely disputed, argument that only those who have undergone some form of personal religious experience are qualified to study religion. The authority of such people thus rests, it is claimed, on their status as 'insiders'. In Units 16 and 17, Section 2, you will meet a comparable argument that only those who appreciate the 'unnatural nature of science' (that is, those with scientific training) are qualified to study historically what scientists do. Let's be clear that these kinds of argument are laid out to be tested, not accepted at face value. You are not being trained in some kind of religious seminary, so the very presence of units on the study of religion in this course immediately implies that there is an alternative way of viewing what students of religion should bring with them. Similarly, you are not required to have a formal scientific qualification in order to read Units 16 and 17. But, as I hope you can already appreciate, both these disciplines in different ways have those within them who *have* insisted on a sharp line being drawn between 'insiders'/practitioners and 'outsiders'/observers. For them, the study of these areas should be left strictly to 'insiders'. In religion, the 'insiders' are those who are able to profess a religious faith, perhaps even testify to some personal transforming experience. Among religious 'insiders', prominence is often given to the specialists – priests, teachers and others who occupy positions of religious authority. In science, the 'insider' is the trained scientist and, increasingly throughout the twentieth century, this came to mean the professional scientist, who was the specialist in his or her field.

The argument that Religious Studies and the History of Science should be left to 'insiders' appears less persuasive, however, when you consider that not only have religious people often violently disagreed about the truths they hold, but that scientists also have a track record of acrimonious disputes over what constitutes 'good' science. Units 16 and 17 offer a case study of one scientist, Alfred Russel Wallace, who was largely dismissed by the scientific establishment of his day. It may be, therefore, that we should be cautious before conceding that authority in these matters should be handed over to 'insiders'. The problem of the authority of the 'insider' takes on significantly larger proportions in the study of religion than in the History of Science because of the difficulties involved in testing religious claims made by insiders, whether for the existence of a deity, the authority of a teacher or sacred book, or the supremacy of one way of life over others. Yet, like religious systems, science also claims to uncover truths about the way the universe works. But even with strictly controlled scientific experimentation (for which there is no parallel in the testing of different religious claims), it may take many years for a consensus to be reached. In the intervening period, unresolved controversy may continue to rage, with all parties appealing to science. Units 16 and 17 invite you to explore one historical process through which scientific consensus has been reached. Even when difficulties such as these are fully recognized, however, we are still left with two areas of human endeavour, religion and science, where participants have insisted that it is only the 'insider' who stands any chance of *really* understanding what lies at the heart of these enterprises. It is this thorny problem that lies at the heart of the discussion of scholarly methods in Block 4.

Block 4 also offers an account of how Religious Studies and the History of Science became established as disciplines in their own right (Units 14 and 15, Sections 4 and 6; Units 16 and 17, Section 2). Both these disciplines have relatively recent origins in the nineteenth century, although their subject matter has a long history. The kind of study of religion that you will meet in Block 4 parted company from theology, which was largely Christian in its outlook, and the History of Science emerged as a discipline concerned with much more than a narrow, internalistic history of scientific ideas and discoveries. These new disciplines arose from the insistence of their early champions that they should be freed from the constraints of having to speak as 'insiders' precisely in order to study 'insiders', the actual practitioners of religion and science, with the same degree of detachment required in other branches of the Humanities.

Finally, the insistence in both Religious Studies and the History of Science upon the need to adopt a different perspective from that of the practitioners of religion or science also leads these disciplines to seek to understand things in context – historical, social and cultural. What may at first sight seem difficult to understand or even alien when viewed from one particular historical/cultural perspective often takes on new meaning when viewed within its own setting. In order to illustrate this point, Units 14 and 15, Section 7 offers a brief study of worship and festival in Calcutta in order to encourage you to reflect on how we use the term 'religion' and how we study those things we label 'religion'. Similarly, Units 16 and 17, Sections 3–7 provide an extended study of the Victorian scientist, Alfred Russel Wallace, whose views about evolution and spiritualism provoked many scientists of his generation but, the units argue, now merit fresh consideration. The choice of material taken from an Indian location in Units 14 and 15 has been deliberate in that it provides an opportunity for you to extend your cross-cultural studies beyond the confines of Europe and North America.

The study of religion and the History of Science may have struck you as an odd couple. In a month's time, you should be able to appreciate how exploring some of the problems that these two disciplines share in common fits into the sequence of critical issues that provide the landmarks on your passage through A103.

UNITS 14 AND 15 STUDYING RELIGION

Written for the course team by Gwilym Beckerlegge

Contents

STUDY WEEKS FOURTEEN & FIFTEEN

STUDY COMPONENTS				
Weeks of study	Texts	TV	AC	Set books
2	*Resource Book 3*	TV14 TV15	–	–

Aims and objectives

The aim of these units is to explore three key questions:

1   Why study religion?

2   What is religion?

3   How should religion be studied?

When you have completed these units, you should:

1   be able to discuss some of the ways in which the concept of 'religion' has been and is used in the study of religion;

2   have gained some practical experience in the study of religion through exploring examples of religious activity in Britain and India on 'special days';

3   be able to identify and to evaluate critically the motives, concerns and methods that typically distinguish the academic study of religion known as Religious Studies from other approaches to religious belief and practice.

You may find it helpful to return to these objectives when you evaluate your progress at the end of these units.

Study notes

These units will introduce you to the study of religion by giving you an opportunity to think about some of the key concepts and methods of the discipline of Religious Studies. You will meet examples of different forms of religious practice and belief, mostly from Britain and India, and will compare the ways in which boundaries are drawn (or not drawn) between what is held to be 'religious' and 'non-religious' in two different societies.

Individuals will work through the sections of these units at different speeds. As a rough guide, you will find Sections 1–3 fairly light, so you may want to treat Sections 1–5 as your target for the first week, leaving

Sections 6–8 for the second week. You will find that the work becomes more detailed as you progress through the units. There is a glossary on p.78 to help you with unfamiliar terms. There are no set books for you to read and there is no audio-cassette for Units 14 and 15.

TV14 on religion in Liverpool is designed to support Sections 1–6 of these units. TV15 relates to Section 7 and offers a study of religion in Calcutta and the celebration of the Hindu festival of Durga Puja – the worship of the Mother Goddess. People with different beliefs speak for themselves in these programmes and so provide you with the 'raw data' of religion as lived. The programmes are intended to provoke reflection and discussion, including disagreement, rather than to offer neat or final answers to the three key questions identified in the aims of these units. *Do make every effort to watch these programmes closely (tape them, if you can, so that you can return to them) and make your own detailed notes on them.* Remember that you can use the related *Audio-visual Notes* like any other part of the course materials as sources of information when writing notes or preparing an assignment.

1 THAT SPECIAL DAY

It's that special day in the week again. People begin to gather, set apart by their passionate convictions and the symbols that bind them together. Some stand by and scoff but the like-minded take strength from each other and stride proudly on, indifferent to those who do not share their commitment. For those caught up since birth (the less sympathetic might say 'indoctrinated') by their elders' commitment and enthusiasm, this is the climax of their week.

How can an observer convey in words the feelings of those who gather at this special place at this special time? The chanting and singing lift those present out of the work-a-day world. Truly, to be here does raise the spirits and charge the batteries for the week ahead. To be sitting in the same row and conscious of familiar faces, possibly among generations of the same family, gives a sense of belonging that others can hardly imagine. This is something of value to be passed from generation to generation. But enough of this; those who will officiate have taken up their positions. It is time for minds and hearts to focus, for the moment has come. The whistle blows, the ball is passed, the match has begun.

My account of 'that special day' deliberately encourages you to assume that I was beginning this study of religion with a description of a religious gathering at a place of worship. After all, for many people the word 'religion' conjures up just such a picture of gatherings on days held to be special by different groups in the community; for example, at a Jewish **synagogue** on Saturday, an Islamic **mosque** on a Friday (Islam is professed by Muslims) and a Christian **church** on a Sunday. Whether or not you think of yourself as religious, the celebration of these special days and the marking of events such as marriage and death in places like churches or mosques are hard to avoid. Regardless of our personal attitudes towards religion, these associations give rise to a measure of shared understanding of what we mean by 'religion'. It's something we take for granted. You might anticipate, therefore, that mapping the limits of 'religion' should be straightforward – a matter of common sense, for we all know what we mean by 'religion'. But is it as straightforward as that?

One prominent football manager declared: 'Some people say that football is a matter of life and death. It isn't. It's much more important than that' (Bill Shankly, when manager of Liverpool Football Club). In speaking about his personal commitment to football, I am sure that Bill Shankly was not intentionally seeking to cast it as some sort of 'religion'. Yet, the language he used is reminiscent of a characteristic associated with 'religion': namely, that 'religion' claims to offer its followers meaning and a way through life which leads them to attach greater importance to it than anything else. If we take Bill Shankly seriously, establishing a clear boundary between religion and other kinds of commitment may prove less easy than we might have imagined.

EXERCISE

Can you suggest some parallels between following a football club and following a religion?

DISCUSSION

Both football and religion can arouse deep passions, even to the point of violence, and their respective followers will often make considerable sacrifices. Both groups are inclined to mark themselves out with exclusive codes of dress and forms of ritual behaviour. Both have their own songs. There is individual experience but also a powerful sense of belonging to a community with its own code, which is reinforced by sharing in pilgrimage – whether to a place of worship or to a football stadium. Both religion and football produce their heroes, their ordinary followers and their fanatics.

FIGURE 14/15.1
*Football supporters show their colours.
Photo: Popperfoto*

So, am I suggesting that the activity of a religious person at a place of worship can be adequately described in much the same way as, for example, the passionate support of a football fan at the local stadium? Not exactly, but I do want you to consider that the meaning of the familiar term 'religion' may be less clear-cut than it seems. Although many people rush to pronounce judgements on whether religion is 'true' or 'false' or whether it is a 'good' thing or a 'bad' thing, few pause long enough to ask, 'what is religion – how do we recognize it when we encounter it?'

2 RELIGION IN THE LANDSCAPE

Everyday perceptions

So, how do we recognize 'religion' when we encounter it? You can answer this from your own experience.

Imagine walking through a town or village centre that you know well and think about the signs of religion that you would see. Simply take your own understanding of the term 'religion' (however vague) as your starting point.

1   What sort of things would catch your attention?

2   Why would you consider these things as having to do with 'religion'?

3   Would you expect anyone to disagree with what you see as signs of 'religion'?

Try to sketch out your answers to these questions with plenty of specific examples.

DISCUSSION

1   If this walk took place in Britain, churches would be likely to catch your eye, possibly the symbolism of the Christian cross, maybe reference on a sign to the name of a group that you associate with religion.[1] Some street names and pub signs have Christian associations. You might meet somebody whose dress carries what you recognize as religious symbolism (for example, the collar worn by a member of the Christian clergy), see decoration, hear music or even catch a scent you associate with religion. I am sure that you will have found many more examples, and not just war memorials!

I have started with Christian symbolism on the assumption that our imaginary walk is taking place in Britain where Christianity has been the dominant tradition for many centuries. It is quite difficult to find inhabited areas where there is not a church tower or steeple somewhere on the skyline (Figure 14/15.2). But if you have been thinking about a larger town, you may well have come up with far more varied list: different expressions of Christianity such as a Quaker meeting house or a Salvation Army citadel, possibly a Jewish synagogue, an Islamic mosque (Figure 14/15.3), or centres of

[1] If you are not resident in Britain, try to apply the general points to your examples.

Buddhist, Sikh or Hindu activity (Figure 14/15.4). You may have listed foodshops, such as a **kosher** delicatessen providing food prepared according to Jewish dietary law, or charity shops connected to organizations such as Christian Aid. At different times of the year, other shops may be selling seasonal items like Easter eggs or festival cards. Styles of dress, such as the turbans worn by male Sikhs, also may bring religious practice to mind. All these examples are part of Britain's contemporary urban landscape.

2   Familiarity is probably the short answer to this question. All of us are attuned to look for signs of the familiar. In this case, it would be forms of religion that you recognize in your society, whether you believe in them personally or not.

3   Others may not agree with how the concept of 'religion' should be defined. Some people, for example, hold strong religious convictions and may not admit that other forms of belief and practice could be placed in the same category as their own. Others may simply not be familiar with some of the examples listed above and would not recognize them. For example, imagine an old school building that had been converted into a Sikh *gurdwara*. This is a place of

FIGURE 14/15.2   *Parish church – Haddenham. Photo: Anthony Coulson*

worship that houses the sacred book of the Sikhs. Although it may not be recognizable as such to someone unfamiliar with the Sikh tradition, it is likely that most people would accept the converted school as a sign of 'religion' once they understood its new purpose. Similarly, someone unfamiliar with the signs of Christianity might assume that the use of a green cross over a chemist's shop carried the same significance as the cross found outside a Christian mission hall. An explanation of the difference between the two symbols would probably move the chemist's shop off any list of 'religious' buildings.

FIGURE 14/15.3   *The purpose-built East London Mosque, Whitechapel. Photo: Carlos Reyes-Manzo/ Andes Press Agency*

FIGURE 14/15.4   *Hindu temple, Greenwich. Photo: Carlos Reyes-Manzo/Andes Press Agency*

Assumptions

We are beginning to see that many of the assumptions we hold about the characteristics of 'religion' are given to us by the society we live in or by our immediate community, which for some people may be a religious community. Don't lose sight of your assumptions about religion. At this point, it may be that you have not thought much about them before, or you may be personally hostile to religion, or be approaching these units from the standpoint of a very specific, personal religious conviction. Later in the units I am going to argue that the study of religion should not be coloured either by personal religious conviction, or lack of it. To argue in this way, however, is not to deny that we all bring assumptions – individual, social and cultural – to any study we undertake. This is an important point that we shall discuss when we examine how to study religion in Section 6. For the moment, I want to continue looking at the way in which the word 'religion' is commonly used and understood.

When dealing with the signs of religion, there would probably be general agreement that Christianity, Hinduism, Islam, Judaism and Sikhism – all

FIGURE 14/15.5
Yoga relaxation class.
Photo: Popperfoto

of which have many followers in Britain – are religions, if for no other reason than because this is how they are conventionally described. (Note that we have slid from talking about 'religion' in general to specific 'religions'; we will come back to this in Section 4.) However, if you had imagined walking into a 'New Age' bookshop, you might have have found yourself juggling with words like 'cult', 'mysticism', 'magic', 'superstition' as well as 'religion'. You might have found yourself pondering whether yoga is more akin to 'religion' than aerobics (Figure 14/15.5), or whether the TM (Transcendental Meditation) classes, which are being advertised at the local college, are an expression of a particular lifestyle or philosophy, a leisure activity, or part of a distinctively religious outlook and practice.

EXERCISE

Please read Eileen Barker's brief account of TM in *Resource Book 3*, A1. It includes a few references to the Hindu religious tradition: a **guru** is a spiritual teacher and this title is given to Maharishi Mahesh Yogi, the founder of TM; *siddhi* is, roughly speaking, a power or heightened ability, and Vedic relates to the **Veda**, the unidentified Hindu scripture referred to at the beginning of the description.

Then turn to *Resource Book 3,* A2, and read the extracts from a book published from within the TM movement. Look also at Figure 14/15.6, which is reproduced from the same book. When you have done that, compare these two viewpoints on the status of TM. Simply on the basis of what these readings present to you, do you think TM is a religion?

As you think about this question, consider carefully the basis upon which you intend to make your judgement. For example, will you rely upon your own assumptions? Or will you be guided more by what TM has to say about itself? What weight will you give to the opinion of Eileen Barker, an expert on new religious movements but not writing from within TM? After answering the question, please write down the factors which most affected your decision about whether TM is a religion.

DISCUSSION

In tackling this exercise, it is unlikely that you were able to draw upon a broadly agreed view of the status of TM. If TM was unfamiliar, you may well have asked if it was anything like a religion that you were familiar with. For Barker, it would seem that the status of TM is clear; for her it is a religious movement. Its founder studied under a guru, who derived the meditation technique from the ancient Hindu tradition. For the TM writers, however, TM is not a religion and certainly not a Westernized form of the Hindu religion. Its connection with India is merely historical. It can be practised by anyone – people of different religions and atheists alike.

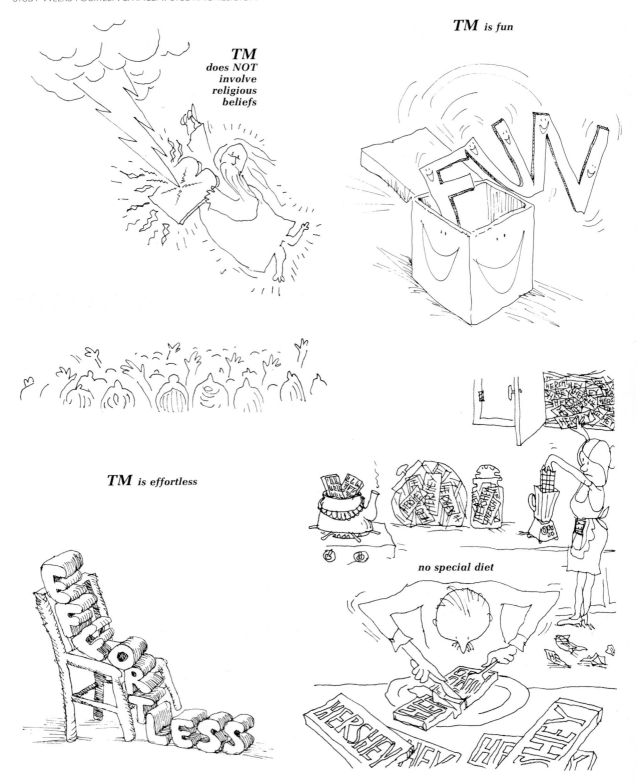

FIGURE 14/15.6 *TM illustrations by Barry Geller. Reproduced from D. Denniston and P. McWilliams,* The TM Book: How to Enjoy the Rest of Your Life, *1975, Michigan, Versemonger Press, pp.14, 20, 44, 48*

Could you resolve this difference in interpretation? You might have felt that the associations with the Hindu religion were too strong to be ignored, but you might also have noticed the statement from the TM leaflet, included by Barker, that says, 'TM requires no belief or any great commitment'. I do not want to press a particular conclusion on you because the exercise is designed to make you aware of *the way* in which *you* tried to reach a conclusion. Do note, however, that TM members themselves have views on this matter. As students of religion, to what extent should we be guided by the views of those we study? Eileen Barker has set aside the opinion held within TM. Can we similarly set aside the view of Jews when we come to the study of Judaism? Or the views of those labelled 'religious' when we analyse the use of the term 'religion'? This is an important question that we shall discuss more fully in Section 6. For now, let's consider some views of other people who are described as having a 'religion'.

EXERCISE

I would like you now to read three extracts in *Resource Book 3* reprinted from John Bowker's book about religion in Britain – A3 'I live by faith: the religions described': (A) Hinduism, (D) Judaism and (F) Islam. Please make thorough notes as you go, writing down the major features of the beliefs and practices described and any major points of similarity and difference that strike you. (Note: TV14 covers these religions within the city of Liverpool. When you have seen the programme, do try to integrate the notes you make on it with your notes on this exercise and do read the *Audio-visual Notes.*)

What do you learn from Bowker's account about the way in which some Hindus, Jews and Muslims react to the use of the term 'religion' when it is applied to their beliefs and practices?

DISCUSSION

One Hindu interviewed by Bowker questioned whether the term 'religion' adequately described his faith, explaining that 'Hinduism is a way of life rather than a religion'. Another claimed that 'Hinduism is not a religion, in the same sense in which Christianity is a religion'. A Muslim explained that Muslims do not refer to Islam as a 'religion' but as a 'way of life'. Bowker suggests that this view would be shared by many Jews when speaking of Judaism.

In TV14 you will see others who were not happy about the unqualified use of the word 'religion' to describe their own beliefs and practices. Some of the speakers preferred 'way of life' or 'faith' rather than 'religion'. A Muslim pointed out that the sacred book of Islam, the **Qur'an**, used the Arabic *din* to refer to Islam which, he stated, was far better translated into English as a 'way of life'. In the minds of some, 'religion' was equated too narrowly with ritual, for others with worship and/or with belief in God. It was because of these sorts of associations that the spokesperson for TM was adamant that it is not a 'religion'. It seems, then, that the use of the familiar term 'religion' is not only problematic in relation to more recent styles of belief and practice (such as TM). It may be disputed even when applied to long-standing beliefs and practices that I am sure most people in Britain would unhesitatingly think of as 'religion'.

Religions in Britain

I would like you to continue your reading of the extracts from John Bowker's account of religions in Britain as it is important that you build up your general knowledge of those beliefs and practices commonly labelled as 'religion'.

EXERCISE

Please read the remainder of 'I live by faith: the religions described' in *Resource Book 3*, A3: (B) Buddhism, (C) Sikhism and (E) Christianity. Again, I suggest that you make notes on the major features of the beliefs and practices described, and also jot down any major points of similarity and difference that strike you. (As before, when you have seen TV14, please integrate your notes on the programme with your notes on the Bowker extract and please read the *Audio-visual Notes*.)

DISCUSSION

All the traditions covered by Bowker and TV14 are referred to as 'religions'. I am sure that you will find both similarities – for example, all of them encourage communal practices such as worship in a special place – and also differences. You might feel that some of these differences are quite minor – merely differences in detail. For example, Sikhs adhere to the visible symbolism of the '**Five Ks**', including uncut hair and the wearing of a steel bangle and symbolic dagger; Jews have a dietary practice; and Muslims a pattern of daily prayer at set times.

These practices make a person's religious identity immediately apparent and mark the followers of these religions apart from each other. It is much harder to spot a Christian simply on the basis of outward behaviour and dress. But are these differences in belief simply differences in detail – variations on the same underlying theme?

EXERCISE

I would like you now to look more closely at two of the 'religions' discussed by Bowker and consider whether there are points of difference so great as to make you question how these examples could both be categorized as 'religion'. Referring to sections (B) and (F) of *Resource Book 3*, A3, please compare and contrast the summaries of Buddhist and Islamic beliefs.

DISCUSSION

Islam anticipates the final divine judgement of the individual. Buddhism regards belief in a personal soul as something to be eradicated. Existence, according to the Buddhist, is a process controlled by strict laws and not presided over by a God upon whom humans depend for their 'salvation'. This seems like a profound difference and not simply a difference in detail.

If Bowker's treatment of both Buddhism and Islam as 'religions' is justified, it also challenges another assumption about religion that is popularly made, at least by many in Europe. This is that all religions, in spite of their differences, share a belief in a God or gods. As you have seen, the Buddhist tradition, which has been influential throughout much of south-east and east Asia, has often been described as 'atheistic' (lacking belief in the existence of an eternal God) and has appealed to many people in Britain and elsewhere for precisely this reason.

Once again we see that the popular conventional use of the term 'religion' is far from straightforward. It refers to a widely differing range of beliefs held by people in Britain. Its popular use implies that there is sufficient in common between Islam and Buddhism to place them within this same overall category of 'religion'. Yet, Islam speaks uncompromisingly about the divine will of **Allah** (God), the creator of all, and Buddhism certainly does not speak of all things coming into being as a result of acts of creation. The popular use of 'religion' nevertheless implies that there is more in common between them than, say, between Christianity and Marxism. We shall have more to say about this in Section 4 when we examine some of the ways in which scholars have responded to the question, 'what is religion?'.

Remember that at the beginning of these units I challenged the view that establishing a boundary line around 'religion' would be straightforward. Anybody can express a view about what kind of a thing religion is, whether they like it or not, and about the extent to which they believe that religion is true. People do this in reacting to news stories, whether about pronouncements from the Archbishop of Canterbury, the veiling of Muslim women, or some little-known sect. One of the purposes of A103 is to introduce you to skills that will enable you to test judgements passed by others and encourage you to become aware of the way in which you arrive at your own judgements. I would call the kind of study that made use of such skills a 'critical study'. This doesn't mean approaching a subject in a negative and destructive spirit. Rather, critical students are those who are led by a spirit of free enquiry and who seek to test their own conclusions, and the claims made by others, in the light of reliable evidence and sound argument. You have already done this in the exercise on TM.

Life is short and yet academics still seem to find the time to take a commonplace term or assumption and turn it into a 'problem'! Why should you want to take on board another 'problem' – that of the use of the term 'religion'? Why study religion in the first place?

3 WHY STUDY RELIGION?

The cart before the horse?

At this point you may be wondering whether you blinked and missed something, or whether I have omitted a crucial step. So far, I have been pressing you to agree that the term 'religion' is crying out for more careful, critical definition. Now I am asking why you should wish to study something that has boundaries you can, apparently, no longer take for granted. Surely, we need to know what the thing is before we can say why we might wish to study it? Yet, when we decide to study something, we often begin with little more than an everyday understanding of the subject. In fact, with a topic such as religion it is almost impossible to separate the definition of the subject from the reasons why one might be interested in studying it.

Yet there is a further complication in the relationship between the questions 'what is a religion?' and 'why study religion?'. This is that people are inclined to take up the study of religion (or steer well clear of it!) on the basis of personal assumptions, not simply about the value of religion but about its truth or falsity. Such people 'know' what religion is, and this is why they study it or ignore it. Even those who do not begin from a fixed view about the truth of religion but take up the study of religion because of its visible effects upon society may well put the question 'what is religion?' on hold; they too at least know why they are studying it and that is a sufficient starting point. However, once you get into the study of religion you tend to realize that the everyday and popular understanding of religion, which was certainly good enough to get you started, needs refining and so you then return to the question 'what is religion?' at a different level – from a critical standpoint. This is what we are doing in these units. Let's look now at possible reasons for studying religion before we return in Section 4 to the question 'what is religion?' from a different angle – that of critical study.

Reasons for studying religion

Identify and jot down reasons that you think might prompt someone to make a study of religion.

DISCUSSION

Here are some reasons in no special order why people might choose to study religion. You may well have thought of others.

1   In order to understand the influence of religion upon art, drama, music and literature.

2   Because of the impact of religion upon global politics.

3   Because religions claim to convey truths by which human beings should live.

4   In order to find a religion to live by or for other reasons relating to personal religious self-fulfilment; for example, to deepen an existing religious commitment, to resolve religious doubt, to find a religion in which to believe.

I expect we would agree that there is a value in studying religion to understand the past and the world in which we live now. Think, for example, about the extent to which works of literature, art, drama and music have drawn upon religious symbolism or have been inspired by religious devotion. Again, particularly since 1979 when the Ayatollah Khomeini came to power in Iran, discussion of 'resurgent Islam' and 'Islamic fundamentalism' has been a part of commentaries on international politics. Some time will have lapsed between my writing this unit and you reading it, and you will probably be able to identify more timely and topical examples of the often explosive relationship between religion and politics than my reference to Islam. In our everyday lives, an understanding of religion also helps to foster good relations between communities and individuals. Employers need to understand the conventions that govern the lives of their employees; teachers need to understand the customs observed by their students. Requests for leave to celebrate festivals and for special dietary provisions can only be anticipated and provided where understanding exists.

But if you look carefully at the list of possible reasons outlined above, I think you will see that they fall broadly into two categories. The first category includes reasons for studying religion in order to understand better the society in which we live, the culture we inherit and the wider world of which we are a part (see 1 and 2 above). The second category includes reasons for studying religion that are bound up with the individual's personal quest for religious self-fulfilment (see 3 and 4 above). We might reasonably expect these two sets of motives for studying religion to result in two rather different kinds of approach to that study. We will pick up this point when we draw some conclusions about how to study religion in Section 6.

According to the first category, one reason why we might want to study religion would be to reach a better understanding of contemporary Britain.

The changing face of belief

The religious life of post-war Britain has become more varied, although Christianity in different forms remains the most influential religion. Yet, the influence of Christianity over British institutions has declined greatly over the last century and a half, although both England and Scotland still retain Established Churches (national churches that have formal links with the monarch and are recognized as the state church). In the post-war period religions other than Christianity, as well as other expressions of Christianity, have made their presence felt. Religious belief and behaviour have become more varied and experimental, with the result that the hold of any one religion has weakened. The range of British 'religious activity' has increased and its boundaries have become less distinct. These considerations bring us back again to the issue of what we mean by 'religion'. This question also bears on judgements about the overall place of religion within society. Until we are able to reach a broadly agreed understanding of what constitutes 'religion', determining the extent of the influence of religion in society will remain hedged with problems. Yet, debates in Britain about controversial matters such as blasphemy laws, religious broadcasting, the religious education of children and Sunday trading have all been peppered with assertions about the extent to which the population is religious and therefore wishes to protect the place of religion in national life. In these debates, everyday and popular understandings of what is meant by 'religion' were very much to the fore. Many have argued that the hold of religion over society is in decline as a result of **secularization** – a historical process through which religious beliefs and institutions lose their social significance. To chart the course of such a process and to test claims that religion is facing an irreversible decline, however, again requires that we begin from an agreed understanding of what 'religion' is, the forms it may take, and crucially the extent to which it may change while remaining 'religion'. Without this, how can we determine whether it has declined in importance?

Religion and social policy

Understanding religious beliefs and practices and what we mean by 'religion' is not merely of academic interest. It is often bound up with social policy and so relates to the rights and privileges of individuals. In Britain, for example, the Church of Scientology has not been allowed to register its centre as a place of worship – the closest an organization can get under British law to being recognized as a 'religion' – and thus it has been refused the tax exemptions granted to religious groups as charitable organizations. Between 1968 and 1980, foreign Scientologists were not allowed to enter Britain if their declared purpose was to further the cause of Scientology.

The Church of Scientology has been a highly controversial movement. I will briefly explain why, but I want to use this controversy primarily as an example of the way in which societies determine what is and what is not 'religion'. The theory of Scientology came from the American science-fiction writer, L. Ron Hubbard, who, in 1950, outlined his theory of '**dianetics**'. Dianetics is a form of therapy designed to purge the individual of '**engrams**' – the accumulated imprints of past unpleasant experiences that disturb the reincarnated spirits (or '**thetans**'), dwelling within human beings. Scientology claims to help the individual by using a therapeutic method developed by Hubbard. The Church of Scientology was created in 1954 in the United States, according to one view, so that Scientology could take advantage of the freedom of religion guaranteed under the American Constitution. Scientologists meet on Sundays at services led by recognized ministers in which taped lectures by L. Ron Hubbard are widely used and take the place of prayers and worship. It is on account of this change from therapeutic system to 'church' that Scientology is often counted as a 'new religious movement'.

For almost two decades in Britain, however, accusations have been levelled against Scientology that it is a commercial rather than a religious concern, that its therapeutic system is based on fraud. In 1968 the then Minister of Health described it as a 'pseudo-philosophical cult' and as 'socially harmful'. It has been accused of being an oppressive and intimidating organization that insists its members separate (or 'disconnect') themselves from family and friends who express hostility towards the movement. In ruling that the custody of children should be granted to an ex-Scientologist mother, rather than to their father who remained within Scientology, a British High Court judge described Scientology in 1984 as 'corrupt, sinister and dangerous' and as a 'cult' (quoted in Beckford, 1985, p.68). Since the 1950s Scientology has developed a global following. Popular Hollywood film stars (Tom Cruise, Nicole Kidman and John Travolta) are known to be members of the Church of Scientology. In spite of the high profile of some of its members, as I write, Scientology continues to be regarded with deep suspicion by governments in Britain, France and Germany where it is held not to be an authentic expression of 'religion'.

Under Australian law, however, Scientology has been registered as a 'religion'. Two of the Australian justices who ruled on the status of Scientology identified two characteristics of 'religion' – belief in a supernatural being, thing or principle and a pattern of behaviour that expressed that belief. On this basis, because of its belief in thetans, reincarnation and its goal to release thetans, Scientology was judged to be a religion. A third judge asserted that there was no single characteristic that could be used in law to identify 'religion' but he too felt that a belief in the supernatural was an important indicator (Beckford, 1985, p.133).

Take the case of TM again. In the United States a legal suit was filed against TM in 1976 to test whether it was, as it claimed, merely a meditation technique and not a religion. At stake was the question of whether, under the secular constitution of the United States, TM could be taught in public high schools and so receive grants of public money. The court's verdict was that TM was a religion, and it pointed to similarities between concepts used by TM and other religious, and specifically Hindu, concepts.

Before you seize on this judgement as a way to resolve the problem posed in the exercise on p.21, look at the way the court justified its refusal of the defendants' request that the court define 'religion':

> Owing to the variety of form and substance which religions may take, the courts have avoided the establishment of explicit criteria, the possession of which indelibly identifies an activity as religious.
>
> *(quoted in Baird, 1982, p.404)*

The differences in the responses to movements like TM and Scientology in Britain, Australia and the United States result in part from legal and constitutional differences between these countries. They also hint at the same underlying problems we encountered when reflecting on the characteristics of 'religion' in Section 2. It would seem that convention, custom and practice tell us what counts as 'religion'. But what if new movements emerge that claim to be 'religious', or if the demands of social policy – as in the case of TM in the United States and Scientology in Britain – require that judgements be made about what is and what is not 'religion'?

As we have seen, there are a number of compelling reasons why we should find out what we mean by religion. We can get to one of these by continuing with Eileen Barker's discussion of 'new religious movements'.

EXERCISE

Please now read the extract in *Resource Book 3*, A4, from Eileen Barker's *New Religious Movements* and then answer the following three questions:

1   Why does Barker think that we need consider the question 'what do we mean by religion?'

2   What problems does Barker meet when she tackles this question?

3   In what ways, if any, does Barker help you to answer this question?

(Note: follow the main lines of Barker's argument; you are not expected to be familiar with or to memorize the details relating to the many groups referred to in the extract.)

DISCUSSION

1   For Barker, it is the 'wave of new religious movements', which have taken shape in the post-war period, that causes her to reflect on the question 'what do we mean by religion?'

2   She points to difficulties in giving a ready answer to this question: some definitions are too narrow, some too broad, and some scholars who have listed characteristics of religion have admitted that not all these characteristics need to be evident for a movement to qualify as a religion. Barker also acknowledges that prejudice and vested interests often cloud the issue.

3   As to whether Barker helps us to answer the question 'what do we mean by religion?', beyond pointing to problems in arriving at satisfactory answers, I personally doubt it. To state that most of the movements to which she refers 'are *religious* in the sense that either they offer a religious or philosophical worldview' hardly clarifies the underlying meaning of the term 'religious'.

It is becoming evident that the question 'what is religion?' is fundamental to the study of religion. As we have seen, answers to this question can have significant practical implications for society. This does not mean that everybody who confronts this question will pursue it critically. Some individuals may go no further than their own religious beliefs for an answer, while some who dismiss religion as a waste of time, in effect, similarly base their very different response on their own beliefs. Creating the mental space in which to pause and to examine rationally and systematically that which we know as 'religion', in a way that does not merely reflect our own personal judgements on the truth and value of religion, is the beginning of the critical study of religion.

4 WHAT IS RELIGION?

I want to begin our closer discussion of the question 'what is religion?' by looking briefly at the history of the use and meaning of the term. You may be surprised to find how recently the word 'religion' has taken on the meanings attached to it today.

'Religion' and 'the religions': two new notions

Contemporary scholars of religion emphasize not merely the cultural breadth but also the antiquity of religious activity. Yet, the term 'religion' as we understand it today is very much a Western concept.

> there are today and have been in the past relatively few languages into which one can translate the word 'religion' – and particularly its plural, 'religions' – outside Western civilization.
>
> *(Smith, 1963, p.18)*

We also need to appreciate that the concepts 'religion' and 'the religions' took on new meanings from the period in the eighteenth century known as the Enlightenment. Prior to that time, European scholars paid relatively little attention to religions other than Christianity except, for example, when dismissing Judaism and Islam as false or devilish. When they spoke of Christianity, they tended to use terms like 'faith' or 'church'. The emphasis of Enlightenment thinking was on the individual applying the tests of reason in all branches of enquiry. This resulted in a questioning of religious authority and provoked stringent criticisms of Christian institutions and profoundly affected the ways in which Christianity, in particular, and ultimately 'religion' in general were considered. It was argued that Christian references to a god and the miraculous should be treated no differently from those found in other cultural traditions. In other words, Christianity was placed alongside other traditions that were thought to be in some way comparable. 'Religion' was seen increasingly as a widespread, if not universal, human activity, of which the 'religions' – including Christianity – were examples. Added to this, of course, European traders, colonists and missionaries were beginning to travel more widely. Information about the beliefs, practices and social organizations of other peoples flowed back into Europe.

A consequence of the expansion of Europe was the naming of several religions found beyond the continent. Previously, European writers had referred to many of these indirectly as 'the religion of' a given people; for example, 'the religion of the Chinese'. The names given to religious traditions found in Asia, such as 'Hinduism', 'Buddhism', 'Confucianism' and 'Taoism', are all European inventions and date from the eighteenth and nineteenth centuries. They are labels applied for the convenience of Europeans and not translations of concepts found within these traditions. In the case of Islam, a designation taken from the Qur'an, the Arabic word *islam* (meaning 'the state of accepting the will of God'), was brushed aside by Europeans and, following earlier Christian practice, replaced by 'Mohommedanism'. This term implies that Islam centres upon the person of the Prophet Muhammad rather than Allah (God). Such a substitution is, in fact, blasphemy for a Muslim, which is why the continuing use of the term 'Mohommedanism' by some non-Muslims causes offence.

So really, it is only since the eighteenth century that the term 'religion' has come to be used as a broad category within which are placed particular expressions of religion, such as Christianity or Judaism. Because the term 'religion' is used to include many different kinds of beliefs and practices across cultures and down through time, establishing the boundary of 'religion' will prove to be difficult. We shall also have to determine what it is that these different beliefs and practices have in common that allows them all to be categorized as 'religion'.

I suggested earlier (p.26) that a 'critical' study of religion is what these units are about. Now we are going to look at three ways in which we might try to answer the question 'what is religion?' from the standpoint of a critical study of religion. We will look in turn at:

1   the kind of answer you might find in a general dictionary;

2   the kind of definitions that scholars of religion offer;

3   a 'dimensional' model of religion.

Before we look at any definitions of religion, we need some sort of checklist that will enable us to test their strengths and weaknesses. The last thing I want to do is to saddle you with a single definition of 'religion'; to do that would be to run the risk of making you less critical in your future studies of religion. But I do want to suggest a way in which you can evaluate the usefulness of *different* definitions of 'religion' and the respective merits of different *types* of definition. The following checklist should help you.

A definition should be:

■   *specific* – its criteria should be clear and distinctive;

■   *flexible* – it should not be so narrow as to be exclusive;

■   *free from prejudice* – it should not merely reflect personal dogmatism or unthinking cultural assumptions.

The 'answer' in your dictionary

EXERCISE

Please now look at the definition of 'religion' given in your dictionary.

1   Do you think that the definition is going to help you when deciding what is or is not religion? Please give your reasons, using the checklist.

2   Would it have helped you to determine the status of TM, for example? Again, please note down the reasons for your answer.

Dictionary definitions are likely to differ in phrasing and length, if not in substance, so you will have to apply the following discussion of the definition I found to that in your own dictionary. The *Concise Oxford Dictionary* says in summary that 'religion' is:

(a) monastic conditions, being a monk or nun;

(b) the practice of sacred rites;

(c) one of the prevalent systems of faith and worship;

(d) human recognition of superhuman controlling power and especially of a personal God;

(e) action that one is bound to do.

1   What strikes me is the extent to which this definition reveals the influence of a Christian heritage in that all of these characteristics are to be found within Christianity but less so in other religions – see (a), (c) and (d). The potentially broadest definition, (d), is closed down with its tail-end reference to a 'personal God'. Definition (b), on the other hand, although not narrowly applicable to a particular religion, is narrow in another way, stressing as it does ritual practice. So, to use our checklist, we might say that these definitions at their most specific are *not flexible* and *not free from prejudice* in the sense that they are tied to one set of cultural assumptions.

2   My conclusion is that this kind of definition is unlikely to help us to characterize 'religion' when it is understood as a varied and worldwide activity. To my mind, therefore, it would have provided a very narrow basis upon which to make a judgement about the status of TM, one way or the other. This is why, when I set the earlier exercise, I did not advise you to look in your dictionary.

The purpose of a general dictionary of the kind we have just consulted is to provide the correct meaning of the word established in terms of its origins and usage. The outcome of the previous exercise suggests that the kind of definition required in a specialized enquiry may need to achieve a different level of precision – although the result may not be so concise!

Scholarly definitions of religion

Scholars offer us many different definitions of religion, but these definitions tend to be of two types. The first *type* is known as a *substantive definition*: that is, a definition that tells us what kind of thing religion is by pointing to its distinguishing characteristic – usually its beliefs and/or practices. We can find an example of a substantive definition of religion in my summary of the definitions found in the *Concise Oxford Dictionary*. Look again at (d) above. According to this definition, religion is the 'human recognition of superhuman controlling power and especially of a personal God'.

This particular example, which we have already found to be narrow, illustrates the major problem scholars find with many substantive definitions that attempt to describe religion in terms of *one* distinguishing characteristic. This substantive definition refers to a superhuman power or personal God; others have portrayed religion primarily in terms of the inner experience of the individual or in terms of the social and organizational aspect of religious life.

The selection of a defining characteristic, upon which a substantive definition of religion depends, often reveals prejudice – perhaps a personal religious (even a denominational) bias or a broad cultural bias. Trying to define religion in terms of *one* kind of belief – for example, the belief in one god – may be understandable within the context of Western Europe, which has been dominated historically by Christianity, but is narrow and inflexible when considering religion as a global phenomenon – Buddhism is a case in point. To define religion in terms of one characteristic practice – for example, prayer – appears equally inflexible once religion is treated as a label for a type of activity found across cultures and since the dawn of human history.

In order to avoid being too narrow and too rigid, many scholars prefer a different type of definition known as a *functional definition*. A functional definition concentrates not on what religion *is* (its beliefs and practices, for example) but on what these beliefs and practices *do* for the individual and the social group – on the needs they fulfil (for example, in providing or contributing to bonding, identity, comfort, and security). One well-known example of this kind of definition refers to religion as 'a system of beliefs and practices by means of which a group of people struggles with the ultimate problems of human life' (Yinger, 1970, p.7).

Here you see that the focus of the definition is not on the substance of the beliefs and practices but on what they *do* for people. Religion, as a means by which human beings struggle with 'the ultimate problems of human life', distinctively responds to questions of meaning and purpose raised most sharply, for example, through our encounters with suffering and death. Other functional definitions speak of religion as providing meaning, as a source of fulfilment, as a means of personal transformation, and as a force for social cohesiveness. The advantage of functional definitions is their flexibility. Their disadvantage is that they are not so helpful in determining where religion ends and something else begins.

This fuzzy, blurring tendency in functional definitions is heightened by references such as the one in our example to 'ultimate problems' – other definitions refer to matters of 'ultimate importance'. In other words, according to these definitions, religion distinctively deals with those things in a person's life that are of such importance that everything else is secondary. This is certainly flexible and inclusive but is it sufficiently specific? Aren't we back to the problem we met in Section 1 when I asked you to consider the difference between following religion and following football? You might say that football hardly offers answers to the 'ultimate problems of life' (if you follow Yinger's definition). But following football does appear to make everything else secondary in the lives of some of its fans. Both these things can be the most important thing in people's lives. It seems that, when we come to definitions of religion, we are likely to face a difficult choice between the specific but narrow, and the flexible but vague. Is there a way around this problem?

A dimensional model of religion

Given the problems of devising a succinct definition of religion, some contemporary scholars have produced broader profiles of religion without claiming to identify one distinguishing characteristic. One example of this kind of approach is the seven-dimensional model of religion proposed by Ninian Smart, a specialist in the study of world religions. Smart argues that, if his model is adequate, 'then we do not need to worry greatly about further definition of religion' (Smart, 1989, p.21). This sounds promising. Let's see whether Smart's model can help us with the problem of answering the question 'what is religion?'.

EXERCISE

Please read 'The nature of a religion' by Ninian Smart in *Resource Book 3,* A5 (A). Make sure that you gain a clear understanding of Smart's model of religion by listing its seven dimensions and by reading carefully his description of each one. When you have done that, you should read the next section of Smart's argument, 'The nature of secular worldviews', A5 (B). Then you will be able to work through the following questions.

1   What do *you* think are the strengths of Smart's approach? When making your assessment remember our checklist: a definition should be specific, flexible, and free from prejudice (p.33).

2   Does Smart help us to distinguish between something that passes the seven-dimensional test and something that just looks a bit like a religion?

DISCUSSION

1   Smart is sensitive to diversity (his model is flexible) and does not attempt to define 'religion' in terms of one characteristic belief and/or practice. His model is designed to be specific, to tell us where religion stops and something other than religion begins.

2   Smart does acknowledge that there would be religions in which one or some of his dimensions are either 'weak' or 'virtually non-existent'. (This is an example of a problem that Eileen Barker mentioned: namely, that some scholars who list the characteristics of religion concede that not all have to be visible in every form of religion – see above, p.31). It is consistent with such a conclusion that he views both religions and secular ideologies as 'worldviews', and he urges that they can and should be studied in similar ways because they 'play in the same league'. However, once we get into the realm of 'it looks like but finally isn't', it becomes difficult to see how to apply the seven-dimensional model in the confidence that others using this model would come to the same conclusion. Perhaps one way to resolve this would be to insist upon the primacy of one 'dimension' or characteristic, but this would take us back into the problem touched on when examining substantive definitions of religion.

For all its positive advantages, Smart's model leaves us with the problem of where to draw our line around religion. He teases us with the question of the relationship between religions and secular ideologies in the same way as I trailed the question earlier about the relationship between attendance at a place of worship and at a football match. Smart speaks of the 'likeness' between religions and secular ideologies, of the 'religious-type function' of secular ideologies – which may be helpful ideas, but we are left with the problem of deciding what weight to give to these factors.

We are now in a position, however, to refine our response to the problem posed by the seeming similarities between devotees at a place of worship and passionate fans at a football match. In terms of *function*, we might wish to argue that a fan's passionate attendance at a football match may be *like* that of a religious devotee at a religious event and that it may fulfil the same social and psychological *functions* (bonding, identity, comfort, security, etc.). We still have to determine whether this makes it a *religious* activity.

Common sense and analysis

Faced with the choice between narrow *substantive* definitions and broad *functional* definitions, we should require any definition to 'fit with broad common-sense reflection' and 'encompass what ordinary people mean when they talk of religion' (Bruce, 1995, p.ix). The definition must also assist in the analysis and explanation of what is being studied. For these reasons, Steve Bruce, who is a leading sociologist of religion, opts for the following *substantive* definition:

> Religion, then, consists of beliefs, actions, and institutions which assume the existence of supernatural entities with powers of action, or impersonal powers or processes possessed of moral purpose.
>
> *(Bruce, 1995, p.ix)*

In referring to common sense and ordinary meanings, Bruce is clearly not saying that a scholarly definition does not offer a considerable refinement of 'common-sense' reflection. But if his definition of religion is rooted in the common-sense meanings shared by ordinary people, this suggests that he is likely to be working with an understanding of religion found in English-speaking European culture. Moreover, he handles these meanings as a scholar standing in the European intellectual tradition. Yet, religion – as we keep noting – takes different forms across cultures. It will be important to ensure that Bruce's definition avoids narrowness and does not reflect cultural assumptions unthinkingly. Bruce sets out to avoid these dangers through a reference to beliefs, actions and institutions that points to the multi-dimensional nature of religion and takes us way beyond the narrowness of the substantive definition I derived from the *Concise Oxford Dictionary*. His definition is specific in referring to a characteristic belief in supernatural entities and impersonal powers, although here too he allows for difference. Certainly, using Bruce's definition, I think we could draw a line between following a football team and attending a church service. Similarly, his reference to 'impersonal powers or processes *possessed of a moral purpose*' would enable us to keep Buddhism within the frame while still being able to draw a line between it and, say, Marxism. Although Marxism looks to the evolution of a better social and economic order, this is to be achieved through historical and economic forces which are not in themselves possessed of moral purpose.

Without taking back what I said earlier about not wanting to force any one definition upon you, in conclusion I should say that I think Bruce is right when he points to the advantages of a carefully constructed *substantive* definition of religion. On the other hand, I would not reject the usefulness of dimensional models of religion as a way of expanding upon an initial definition such as that offered by Bruce. Contrary to Ninian Smart, I tend to the view that a dimensional model of religion is likely to prove inadequate when taken by itself. When used in combination, however, a substantive definition and a dimensional model of religion are likely to be far more helpful than broader *functional* definitions when it comes to testing for a boundary between religion and other things that are said to resemble religion: for example, Scientology, football, TM or secular ideologies.

Let me illustrate the usefulness of working with both a substantive definition and a dimensional model of religion in the next section by considering briefly some examples of 'religious' beliefs and practices found in contemporary Britain. I will refer largely to Christian, Jewish and Muslim beliefs so you should reread or check your notes on the accounts of these religions in Bowker's 'I live by faith: the religions described' (*Resource Book 3,* A3). (You will also find it helpful to relate the next section to TV14 when you have seen it.)

5 RELIGION IN CONTEXT: SPECIAL DAYS IN BRITAIN

Whatever else they may be, religions grow in historical and social settings. The present form of a religion has its roots in the past. Religion can exercise a strong influence upon society and the cultural forms of a society, but religion itself is no less affected by changes and pressures within society. Religion gives meaning to a pattern of living and may even be responsible for establishing a certain lifestyle or distinctive social organization or institution. At the same time, religion often works upon symbolism, customs and ideas already to be found in society. In short, a religion exists within a context and can no more be understood adequately apart from that context than can a single line of verse ripped out of a sonnet. Clearly, some of the differences we find between religions, and in the same religion viewed over a period of time, are a result of their development within different historical and social contexts.

In looking at special days in Britain, we will undertake the first of two studies of religion. In this first study, the context I wish to examine is the place of these special days within their immediate religious setting rather than in the wider context of British society. In the second study (in Section 7) I will look more closely at the relationship between expressions of religion and their social context in the city of Calcutta.

Many religions follow weekly and annual cycles of celebration. The official British calendar is marked by both Christian and secular celebrations. In some cases, days that were once Christian celebrations have become secular public holidays; Whitsun is now the Spring Bank Holiday. The celebration of Christmas has become overlaid with customs that have grown in popularity since the Victorian period, so today Christmas trees and the figure of Father Christmas are inseparably linked in the minds of many with the celebration of the birth of Jesus. Attitudes to Sunday, once reserved by Christians as a day of rest and worship, have also changed.

Religions in Britain other than Christianity have their own cycles of celebration, although their days have no place within the list of official British holidays. The Christian day of rest has its roots in the Jewish **Shabbat** (the Sabbath day), the seventh day on which, according to the **Bible**, God rested from the labours of creation. Jews, however, celebrate Shabbat from Friday sunset to Saturday sunset. Muslims are obliged to carry out a cycle of five daily prayers of which the midday prayer on Friday is of particular communal importance to men. Some communities, such as Hindus and Sikhs, are not bound to a weekly pattern of communal worship on a particular day and so have tended to adopt Sunday in Britain. These patterns of celebration are examples of Ninian Smart's *social and institutional dimension*. As you read, try to find further examples of Smart's seven dimensions in addition to those I have highlighted.

The separating out of a special day or time in the week runs in parallel with the marking out of a space that is set aside for worship, ritual and communal activity (*material dimension*). The place where a religious community gathers speaks powerfully about the convictions shared by its members.

FIGURE 14/15.7   *Interior of mosque in Regent's Park, London, showing Muslims at prayer facing the* mihrab. *Photo: Carlos Reyes-Manzo/Andes Press Agency*

This is nowhere more evident than in the mosque where Muslims form orderly lines at the set times of prayer facing a ***mihrab*** (Figure 14/15.7), an empty niche indicating the direction of the city of Mecca to which all Muslims are expected to make a pilgrimage at least once in their life, if they have the health and means to do so. Prayer is led by an ***imam*** ('leader') who stands facing the *mihrab* and who may also give an address during the Friday midday prayer. A typical mosque is singularly lacking in adornment, apart from Arabic calligraphy, and no human figure is portrayed as it is believed that it is blasphemous to attempt to reduce God (Allah) to human form. Muslims believe that the line of prophets recognized by Jews and Christians included Jesus and culminated in the life of Muhammad. Strict Muslim belief insists upon the humanity of these prophets including Muhammad, the greatest of them, to whom was revealed the Qur'an. The Qur'an and the religious laws derived from it provide comprehensive 'guidance' which, if followed, will enable the devout Muslim to meet the test of the Day of Judgement. Individuals who perform the physical ritual of prostration that accompanies prayer symbolize an intent to conform their will to the will of Allah expressed in the Qur'an (*practical and ritual dimension*). The word 'mosque', in fact, comes from the Arabic meaning 'a place of prostration'.

FIGURE 14/15.8   Interior of Whitefield synagogue, Manchester, showing the ark. Photo: Jewish Telegraph Group of Newspapers, Manchester

If the eye is drawn to the *mihrab* in a mosque, in a Jewish synagogue it is drawn to the ark which contains the scroll of **Torah** ('teaching') on which is written what Jews accept as the revelation granted to the patriarch, Moses. (The same scriptural record is to be found in the first five books of the Christian Old Testament.) An ark may be no more than a bare cupboard but the ark in a synagogue is often decorated (Figure 14/15.8). In front of the ark burns the eternal flame. A synagogue (literally, a gathering place) is not a consecrated area. Its primary function is as a place in which to study and receive teaching about the meaning of Torah, and it is the primary duty of a **rabbi**, a qualified teacher of Jewish law, to provide this instruction. Contained within Torah are the ten commandments that insist upon the existence of one God and prohibit any attempt to represent this God in the form of an image (*ethical and legal dimension*). The decoration of a synagogue scrupulously follows this prohibition. For the Jew, to live in accord with the teachings of Torah is to keep faith with a view of history founded upon a belief in a relationship between God and the people of Israel. It anticipates the coming of the **Messiah** (the 'Anointed One' of God) and the inauguration of an age of universal peace. The past sufferings of the Jews have frequently been interpreted within the framework of belief in this relationship with God and in the ultimate realization of the Messianic Age (*narrative or mythic dimension*). The keeping of Shabbat is but one example of living a life designed to fulfil the requirements of Torah and so hasten the coming of the Messianic Age. As is made plain in TV14, the home and not the synagogue is the most important location for celebrating and observing Shabbat.

FIGURE 14/15.9   Interior of St Anselm's Church, Southall, where the symbolism of the cross is prominent in the mass being celebrated. Photo: Carlos Reyes-Manzo/Andes Press Agency

In a Christian place of worship, the style and level of decoration will vary considerably according to the denomination. But whether through the symbolism of a bare cross or an ornate crucifix, with the figure of Jesus hanging from the cross, or through stained glass windows, those present will be directed to the central Christian belief that God took human form in the person of Jesus (Figure 14/15.9). The cross is outlined in the ground-plan of many churches, and other architectural features, such as spires pointing to the heavens, make theological statements of their own. The self-sacrifice of Jesus on the cross provides a model for daily conduct, and the reading of the Bible brings this constantly to mind. In some **Protestant** churches, a prominent place is given to the pulpit, from where the meaning of the Bible is expounded (*doctrinal and philosophical dimension*). In many Christian denominations, the significance of Jesus' death is brought home to believers through the sharing of bread and wine in a manner commended in the Christian New

Testament but understood and carried out in different ways across the denominations. The frequency and importance given to this celebration at the altar also affects the ordering of space within a church, and you will see this if you visit a **Roman Catholic** church where the altar occupies a prominent position and the sharing of bread and wine (the mass) is celebrated daily. If you then go to a nonconformist church or chapel, for example a United Reform Church, there you will probably find that a plain table has replaced an altar, that there is a prominent pulpit, and that the sharing of bread and wine – here referred to as Holy Communion – may take place no more than once a month. The sharing of bread and wine in the name of Jesus is variously believed to stand as a remembrance of his sacrifice (as found widely in Protestantism) or as a mystery through which the bread and wine are transformed into the body and blood of Jesus (as in Roman Catholicism).

Solid objects, whether a cross, an ark or a *mihrab*, can point to something beyond themselves: to a reality which the believer holds to be ever-present yet which cannot be apprehended in the same way as we can hear the chanting of Torah in a synagogue, touch the bread and wine consumed by Christians, and see a Muslim community gather for prayer (*experiential and emotional dimension*). The existence of this reality cannot be established through reference to factors other than the testimony of those who claim to have experienced it. It is for this reason that religion is rejected by some with as much passion as that displayed by its most devout followers. Yet, so compelling is the sense of this reality that it directs and gives meaning to the daily lives of believers.

This brief summary of Muslim, Jewish and Christian practices provides many concrete examples (as I hope you found) of Smart's 'dimensions' or 'aspects' of religion. They also match Bruce's substantive definition in that they are beliefs, actions and institutions that assume the existence of a supernatural entity. The marking out or setting apart evident in these practices is a common feature in many religions.

EXERCISE

Note down some simple physical actions performed by people who enter a church, synagogue or mosque that illustrate this 'marking out' or 'setting apart'. (TV14 will be helpful for this exercise.)

DISCUSSION

Many religions insist that those entering their respective places of worship follow certain codes of dress and/or perform rituals relating to hygiene. For example, although attitudes have become more relaxed of late, many Christians attending a church still choose to wear their best clothes, and women in some denominations prefer to cover their heads while men are expected to remove any head covering. In contrast, Jewish men are careful to cover their heads in a synagogue, whereas Muslims remove their shoes and complete a simple ritual of washing before entering a mosque, and women cover their heads, arms and legs. The practices differ but the underlying intention is the same: to conduct oneself appropriately or respectfully in a place set apart for a distinct purpose. Placing these customs in context enables us to see the underlying purpose. For example, a British Jew who covers his head does so as a mark of humility – the cap is a constant reminder that there is a greater being above humanity. A British Christian who removes his hat before entering church stands in a different tradition in which uncovering the head is a mark of respect and humility.

The tendency within religious behaviour to set things apart from the everyday does not just apply to time and place but also to ideas of authority (leaders and texts), to beliefs more generally, to institutions and to aspects of behaviour as, for example, in dress and diet. In fact, the concept of 'religion/religious' is often set over and against the concept of the 'temporal' and the 'secular', which both suggest an outlook that is concerned solely with this world, the here and now (see above p.28). Yet, religions too are clearly concerned with this world. A religious attitude, however, tends to view this world in relationship to a reality that is not confined by time and space. Some people, as Bruce states, view this reality as a supernatural entity or being (God) whilst others speak of impersonal powers or processes (p.37). Both groups work out their daily behaviour in the light of their beliefs about this unseen reality.

The practice of 'setting apart' or 'marking out' is one consequence of acknowledging the existence of a reality that can in some way be experienced in the here and now and yet goes beyond the here and now. Whatever is particularly associated with this reality, however portrayed, takes on an additional quality. It becomes 'holy' or 'sacred' and is regarded and treated differently from the everyday.

The term 'holy' has commonly been used to describe God, the attributes of God and persons or things associated with God, and carries with it rather narrowly Christian overtones. To speak of something as 'holy' also tends to imply a personal affirmation on the part of the speaker. The term 'sacred' can be used more flexibly. The distinction between the 'sacred' and the 'profane' originally referred to the difference between what took place within the restricted area of a Roman temple (that which was walled off or set apart) and that which was open to all in the area in front of the temple. Today, 'sacred' is normally applied to respected or venerated objects. It describes the attitudes of human beings to these objects rather than making a claim about the reality to which these objects point: for example, sacred beliefs, sacred books, sacred places and, indeed, sacred days. To revert to Bruce, a thing may be 'sacred' because it is associated with a supernatural entity (or entities) or because it is associated with impersonal powers and processes (1995, p.ix).

But if devotees insist that the religious life is to be practised at all times and in all places, then what is the purpose of special gatherings in sacred places? This is a question discussed by Christians, Jews and Muslims in TV14. Some stated simply that it is a requirement of their faith that they mark the week in a certain way. For Muslim men this entailed attending midday Friday prayer at the mosque, for Jews the observance of Shabbat, and for Christians Sunday worship. A fuller answer included the idea that this special event in the week helps the individual to concentrate on the underlying reality of their faith amidst the bustle of the working week. Both Jews and Muslims suggested that men, in particular, were liable to distraction and thus in need of the routine of communal prayer to bring their minds back to God. It was also made plain that the attitudes fostered during this special time in the week should guide the individual for the whole of the week.

To conclude, our brief description of religious practices in Britain reminds us that, if we wish to understand religion, we have to bear in mind the nature of the underlying reality to which religion in its various forms points. Participating in special days, such as the ones we have considered, is held to bring the believer into closer relationship with this reality.

6 HOW SHOULD WE STUDY RELIGION? SOME BASIC PRINCIPLES OF RELIGIOUS STUDIES

Remember that in Section 3 I suggested that possible reasons for studying religion could be clustered together under two broad headings (pp.27–8):

1   to understand the society in which we live, the culture we inherit and the wider world of which we are a part;

2   as part of a personal quest for religious self-fulfilment.

I also suggested that these different reasons might lead to different approaches to the study of religion.

To a great extent, the meanings now attached to the terms 'religion' and 'religions' have tended to promote the study of religion in order to understand the world in which we live rather than as part of a desire for personal religious self-fulfilment. In fact, the assumptions contained within this 'modern' use of 'religion' and 'religions' in themselves indicate something of the approach we must follow. Awareness of the breadth and variety of 'religion' suggests a need:

1   for care when looking for the boundaries of religion;

2   for openness to the variety of possible religious expressions;

3   to place forms of religion in their social and historical context;

4   to avoid premature judgements when dealing with questions about the truth and value of particular religions.

If we are studying religion to make sense of social customs and political events, we can do that without having to make assumptions about the nature of religion, its origins, whether it is a 'good' or 'bad' thing and, whether it is true or false. It is sufficient that people speak about religion as a factor that affects their lives. We can choose to approach these aspects of religion in a neutral manner – that is, without intending to offer any judgement on their truth or falsity. In practice, of course, it is not possible to achieve a position of complete neutrality, but the conscious desire to minimize distortion and bias as far as possible has been a principle adopted in many branches of scholarship. You will already be familiar with this in the reporting and analysis of politics. Certain journalists and commentators evidently strive to be 'disinterested ('impartial' as distinct from 'uninterested') and not to base their judgements on their own political convictions. Even so, at times their impartiality is called into question, particularly by the major political parties in the run-up to an election! Nevertheless, we know that these reporters are attempting to offer a different kind of judgement from those newspaper columnists who make no secret of their political sympathies and write opinion columns that trumpet their convictions. Similarly, the position of the impartial political commentator is significantly different from that of those senior, often retired, politicians who are invited to comment as a result of their vast experience and knowledge of the political process. Retirement may make for greater freedom in criticizing one's own party, but, as viewers, listeners or readers, we know that these figures still speak as 'insiders' and that there are likely to be limits to the extent of their impartiality.

In the study of religion there is a comparable divide. There are those whose style of approach and methods are closely bound up with their own religious convictions or with a personal search for religious self-fulfilment. There are others who, regardless of whether they are religious or not, strive for an impartial approach not shaped by their own beliefs. This latter approach to the study of religion, sometimes known as Religious Studies, has developed in step with the understanding of the terms 'religion' and 'religions' that we have inherited from the late eighteenth century. It is still a relatively new way of studying religion and, in fact, only gained a foothold in European universities in the latter half of the nineteenth century, where it offered an alternative to theology. It also very much the product of the European and North American intellectual traditions.

Religious Studies as a discipline

Until the late nineteenth century, theology had provided the main academic discipline in European universities for the study of religion. Theology (from the Greek, 'discourse about God') is concerned with questions relating to the relationship between God (or gods) and humanity. A theologian may begin from what is held to be a divine revelation taken, say, from a sacred book or religious teacher, about the nature of God and the relationship of God to humanity. In this form, theology is concerned with the interpretation of the substance and implications of a particular revelation. Some styles of theology have relied upon rational reflection upon experience, including observation of nature, in order to formulate beliefs about the nature of God and the relationship between God, the world and human beings. Theological enquiry may be conducted in a highly scholarly manner, and some contemporary theologians argue that its starting point requires nothing more than a willingness to consider the possibility of the existence of God. More typically, however, theology has been practised within the framework of a given religious position. Much of what has gone under the heading of theological training has been shaped by the interests of religious faith and designed to be put to the service of that faith. Historically in Europe it has largely taken the form of Christian theology.

I would certainly agree with you if you reacted to the notion of 'neutral' or disinterested study of religion by arguing that it would be pretty pointless to approach religion in a way that cuts out those parts that might challenge you directly. When you study religion, you do place yourself in a position in which your personal views *may* be changed. Yet, in this respect, the study of religion is no different from other branches of study that examine human ideas and actions, although religious claims are different from those made, say, by political theories. However, a study of religion that *sets out* to deepen an individual's faith, resolve personal religious doubts, or satisfy a need for religious belief is surely a religious quest *in itself.* It could all too easily slide into something entirely directed by that individual's interests: a study within fixed horizons. Even when not restricted to one religious tradition, it is likely to begin with built-in assumptions about the value of religion – for example, that religion in some way provides insights that we have to understand and live by in order to experience a fulfilled existence. Theology has been criticized for fixing the horizons of the study of religion in just this sort of way.

Unlike theology, the interests and methods of Religious Studies are not rooted within the framework of a particular religion. In separating the study of religion from the student's personal religious faith, or lack of faith, Religious Studies has justified its existence on the grounds that religion is a sufficiently distinctive and widespread aspect of human activity as to warrant its own form of enquiry; it does not depend upon assumptions made about either the truth or falsity of religion.

Models of religion, such as that outlined by Ninian Smart (p.36), display the many-sidedness and varied nature of religion. Religious Studies draws upon methods from both the humanities and the social sciences in exploring the complex phenomenon of religion – its history, its art, its ideas, its distinctive social institutions and the states of mind to which it can give rise. Archaeology, comparative methods, history, linguistic studies, pyschology and sociology are all employed within Religious Studies. Religious Studies, therefore, is not founded upon the use of one characteristic method of enquiry but uses a range of different methods to explore a particular area of interest, namely, religion.

Approaching religion as a distinctive and widespread form of human activity implies that we can study religion on broadly the same basis as other human activities. It suggests that, drawing upon common human experiences and our imagination, we can gain insights into what we have not experienced directly. These capacities are used in the same way by historians to help them to reconstruct times past, by anthropologists in the study of societies different from their own, or by actors when they take on a role. There are, however, problems lurking beneath the surface of this brief summary of the broad principles of Religious Studies. The first of these relates to the claim that students of religion can achieve an understanding of religions of which they have no personal experience.

'Insiders' and 'outsiders'

The claim that it is possible to study religion adequately from a disinterested position has been hotly debated. Can the understanding of the observer achieve the same level of insight and authority as the participant in a religion? No serious student of religion can avoid confronting this question.

The 'outsider' cannot escape depending to an extent upon insights from 'insiders' when studying a particular religion. An 'outsider' who has never been through a particular ritual, for example, can only give an account based upon observation and third-party testimony. Observers may be more inclined to rely upon abstractions and generalizations, possibly from sacred books, in the absence of direct experience of the religion as practised. Such questions as 'What does it feel like?' or 'Why did you?' can only be answered by 'insiders' because they call for answers based on personal experience or ask for details that may have to do with a local or even family custom. Yet, 'insiders' are fallible and may have their own reasons for describing their experience in a particular way. 'Insiders' will not necessarily agree with each other.

There is also the further issue of whether the experience of one religion contributes to understanding other forms of religion. For example, does personal experience of the practice of prayer in one religion make a student more sensitive when studying prayer or a practice like meditation in a different religion? Is a Muslim who prays better qualified to understand a Buddhist who meditates and vice versa, than, say, a humanist who does neither? Or should students who are not members of the religion being considered simply be regarded as 'outsiders', whether they are agnostics or members of a different religious faith? Would someone standing outside all religions, but interested in their study, bring an openness and sympathy that a person with a particular religious commitment would find hard to match? If you decide that we should not generalize and that it will depend upon the skill and sensitivity of each student, then you are tacitly accepting that being religious in itself is not a necessary qualification for a student of religion.

In fact, as we have seen, that is one of the principles involved in the approach of Religious Studies. Fervent followers of religion and militant atheists both have the capacity to become insightful students of religion – as long as they are willing to exercise the self-discipline necessary to ensure that their own beliefs do not distort their treatment of the beliefs of others. If I did not accept this possibility, introducing you to Religious Studies would be tantamount to assuming either that you are religious or that you will need to 'get religious quick' to complete this part of A103! Yet, the argument that it *is* possible to study religion effectively without drawing upon personal religious experience has been challenged.

The counter-argument is that 'religion' refers to a totally distinct and unique category of human experience which is beyond the comprehension of those who have not shared this experience. A technical way of referring to this is to speak of religion as being **autonomous** (subject to its own laws) or as being *sui generis* (Latin for 'of its own kind' or unique and pronounced as 'soo-ee g[hard 'g' as in gun]en-er-is'). The implications of this view for the student have been spelled out in no uncertain terms:

> The reader is invited to direct his mind to a moment of deeply-felt religious experience, as little as possible qualified by other forms of consciousness. Whoever cannot do this, whoever knows no such moments in his experience, is requested to read no further; for it is not easy to discuss questions of religious pyschology with one who can recollect the emotions of his adolescence, the discomforts of indigestion, or, say, social feelings, but cannot recall any intrinsically religious feelings.
>
> *(Otto, 1970, p.8)*

According to this view there are severe limits to the extent to which religion can be understood by the 'outsider' who has not known 'intrinsically religious feelings'. This would seem to rule out, for example, Ninian Smart's argument that both religions and secular ideologies should be studied as 'worldviews' (p.37). For if religion is different in kind from a secular **ideology**, then it cannot be understood on the same terms as other 'worldviews', but only on its own terms by those who have known some sort of religious experience of their own.

Is acceptance of the claim that religion is autonomous or *sui generis* consistent with the broad principles of Religious Studies?

We might wish to investigate the claim that religion is autonomous or *sui generis* as part of our study of religion. To base our method of study on the acceptance of such a claim without first testing the arguments that support it, however, would be to begin from an assumption that is very different from the characteristic but more modest starting point of Religious Studies: namely, the observable importance of religion in peoples' lives. Yet, we should be aware of the implications of rejecting the *sui generis* argument. In so doing we *have* made a statement about the nature of religion: that, for the purposes of study, we are assuming that it is possible to study religion in much the same way as we study other aspects of human experience. On the other hand, those who view religion as *sui generis* face the problems of identifying what makes it so (which, given the varied forms of religion, is not easy), and also of convincing us that a person who has experienced one form of religion may apply this experience in the analysis of another.

The difference of opinion between those who hold to the *sui generis* view of religion and those who share the position adopted by Ninian Smart is profound. The fact that the debate continues leads us into another problem in the study of religion in response to which Religious Studies has adopted a characteristic position in terms of method. This is the problem of determining the truth of religion.

Religion: true or false?

I noted above that differences between the truth claims made by religions has led those who practise Religious Studies to avoid premature judgements when dealing with questions relating to the truth and value of particular religions. By seeming to by-pass truth claims, you may feel that what I have been describing as Religious Studies avoids what many would regard as the purpose of religion – to deal in truths. This is a difficult area to cover briefly, but let me at least try to explain why Religious Studies takes the line that it does.

Different societies tolerate different codes of morality. Religions, which typically claim to reveal truths, often make different claims and promote different codes of behaviour. Can we just assume that these variations are due to the differences in the social and historical contexts in which these religions are found? Some people have argued that *all* religions contain a measure of certain universal truths, but have taken different outward forms because of the needs of different human temperaments and different social conditions. In Section 7 we shall see that some contemporary Hindus are wedded to this idea. There is even an old Indian story used to illustrate it. Wearied by the conflicting opinions of his court philosophers and their mutual intolerance, a king made them watch blind men approach an elephant from different angles and, using their sense of touch, attempt to identify what creature they were being presented with. Not surprisingly, the blind man who grabbed the tail arrived at a different conclusion from the one who embraced a leg. At one level this story serves to encourage humility when asserting one's opinions, but the story has also been used to suggest something about the relationship between religions that could guide the way we study them.

EXERCISE

Think about the Indian story I have just related:

1   What appears to be its message about conflicting religious and philosophical beliefs?

2   Does the message of the story provide guidelines that we might adopt in our role as critical students of religion?

DISCUSSION

1   The story implies that nobody has a monopoly on truth. Humans are like the blind men – we have a limited perception of the universe. But the story also suggests that while the blind men did not grasp the complete picture, they all had some insight. The story invites us to understand the reasons for their failure and not to judge them intolerantly as the court philosophers had judged each other.

2   The plea for tolerance and respect may sound attractive, but it does not take us much further forward in deciding how to deal with questions of truth. In the terms of this story, all religions are true in their own way and are thus to be respected for meeting different needs. But this is where we do hit a problem. The story presupposes that the elephant *was* there and that, even when wrong in their conclusions, the blind men had grasped something of the larger picture. Put the pieces together, learn from each other and you will have the right answer. Transferring this to the study of religion would imply that students assume *for the purposes of their method* that all religions are true in some measure. This may make for tolerance and respect, but it is as much a judgement on the truth claims of religion as are the assumptions that one religion is true or that none are true. For this reason, I feel that the story makes us think harder about how to study religion rather than providing us with a model answer.

The problem is that, in the study of religion, there is no human arbiter comparable to that of the sighted in the story of the blind men and the elephant. Truth claims – for example, about the existence of God – are made within particular religions, and it is between religions that the differences lie. Religions start, however, from different assumptions and appeal to different authorities. Finding a way that will enable us to judge the respective merits of their truth claims is, therefore, extremely difficult. For example, religious traditions often appeal to a sacred book whose authority is not recognized either by people of other faiths or by people of no religious faith. Those who accept the authority of a sacred book are unlikely to accept the judgements of those who deny its authority.

Arguments used to set out and justify religious claims may be tested in the way that was demonstrated in Unit 4. You may remember that one of the examples used there was an argument against the existence of God (Block 1, pp.146–8). But religious conviction, even when it appeals to reason and logic, more often than not assigns a greater importance to acts of faith, to personal experience and/or to the authority of a religious teacher or sacred book. A person whose conviction rests on foundations such as these may well turn round and argue that an outsider who attempts to judge the truth of a particular religion without such an experience simply does not understand the religion and is thus simply not qualified to judge its truth claims. I remember well talking with a Muslim who has generously given of his time over several years to answer my questions about Islam. On one occasion when we were outside the mosque talking about understanding Islam, he turned to me and said simply, 'If you understood Islam, you would come into the mosque with me now and make your profession of faith'.

Trying to resolve the problem of how to test religious truth claims continues to vex scholars and religious devotees alike. Those who practise Religious Studies recognize the full importance of this problem, but do not believe that all study of religion should be suspended until it is solved. We continue in the meantime to learn more about religion, but refrain from making premature judgements about matters of truth. In view of the amount of biased and inaccurate reporting of religions which has taken place and continues to take place both in the media and in scholarly work, a measure of caution about premature judgements may be no bad thing. To an extent, this also offers a check when applying the assumptions, principles and methods of Religious Studies, a discipline that evolved in post-Enlightenment Europe, in a global, cross-cultural study of beliefs and practices. But does this mean we can offer only bland descriptions of religion and no evaluative comment? Doesn't religion on occasion actually do damage?

Religion: a 'good' thing or a 'bad' thing?

In considering the value of religions, we can begin by saying that one of the first tasks of the critical student should certainly be to test the basis of judgements offered by other commentators. We saw earlier that the Church of Scientology has had problems gaining official recognition as a 'religion' in a number of countries and that these judgements have been tied up with official views that Scientology is 'socially harmful'.

Dramatic events like those surrounding the mass suicide of a religious group or an armed stand-off between a religious group and a government agency need to be understood and explained. To this end, students of religion use methods of historical, psychological and sociological investigation. Sociological and psychological analysis may also help us to understand why individuals are drawn into religious movements and the effects of joining upon both them and their families. This is a particularly pressing question for those who have seen a relative or friend become part of a religious community that closes its members off from those who do not share the same beliefs.

Similarly, claims made about the effects of different techniques of meditation are open to a degree of clinical testing. Many clinical tests have been carried out to measure the effects of different meditative techniques upon rhythms in the brain and upon blood-pressure. In examining this kind of evidence as critical students, we may be acting little differently from someone who is considering taking up a meditation practice but who first wants to know whether it can bring benefits.

To argue, as I have done, that Religious Studies stresses the need to understand beliefs and practices in their context is not to say that the student may offer no judgement upon these. As we have seen, many of the practical consequences of religious codes of conduct are open to observation and investigation, and the justifications for different codes can be tested for coherence. The judgements we pass, however, should be informed by understanding this behaviour within its historical and social context, and not simply exercised on the assumption that our own moral code provides a universal standard against which all else may be judged. Think, for example, about the way in which monogamy and polygamy have been regarded as the norm in different societies. Similarly, the age at which it is thought appropriate for young people to enter into full sexual relationships varies considerably. So, although one society might seek to promote or even enforce one standard, as critical students we have to recognize that such standards do vary, and often for good reason, between societies.

EXERCISE

In the light of what has just been said, are there claims made or issues relating to the lifestyles described in TV14 and TV15 that you would want to subject to more searching, critical enquiry? Please identify at least one issue in these programmes and list two or three questions you would want to pursue. (If you have not seen the programmes, please relate this question to your reading from Bowker in *Resource Book 3,* A3.)

DISCUSSION

There are many issues that you might have listed. This is one example that caught my attention because it surfaced a number of times. Whether in Britain or in India, the religions that figured in the programmes appeared to offer women a more restricted role in the life of the community. In certain instances, communal worship was largely if not exclusively centred upon the needs of men and key roles seemed to be reserved for men. This was evident in the roles played by men as priests in Christian churches, even though women are now ordained in some denominations. While it was claimed that women were more innately religious than men, often in practice they seemed to be confined to subordinate roles whether in the home or elsewhere. Jews and Muslims downplayed the need for women to attend communal worship and prayer. In Calcutta the domestic role undertaken by Hindu women was likened to a service offered up to the deities. What part does religion play in the social construction of the roles assigned to the two sexes? What effects has this had upon the lives of men and women and their respective places within society? Is this influence different from social convention more generally, or does religion play a major hand in creating and maintaining social conventions? These are the sorts of question that we should be asking as critical students. I think I would also want to ask further questions about the meaning and value that religious people assign to these roles as a prelude to attempting to answer my other questions.

Religious Studies, then, is not simply a mix of bland and evocative description, but is concerned to understand and analyse the part that religion plays in the lives of people. Our current inability to resolve which religions, if any, are true is a source of frustration but it also vitalizes the discipline. After all, if we knew the answer to this question, we would probably be at the end of our need to study religion and some of us would be out of a job. This limitation should make for humility but not paralysis. Religious Studies is not the only discipline you will meet in A103 where questions of truth remain to be resolved.

Now that we have a clearer view of the concerns of Religious Studies and some of the problems associated with using the term 'religion', I want to move beyond the confines of British society and shift our attention to India and the religious tradition widely known as 'Hinduism'. We are taking this as our next example because Hinduism historically has taken many different forms, and thus defining Hinduism as a 'religion' poses particular problems. Taking the different contexts of India and Britain should also make us less inclined to slip into an unthinking acceptance of the assumptions made about religion in one culture and about how to study it. I realize that some of you may know Hindu India well, but my discussion assumes that this will be unfamiliar territory for the majority of you. During this more extended study of religion in context, you will have the opportunity to get a fuller flavour of studying religion and to practise some of the skills you have developed up to this point.

7 RELIGION IN CONTEXT: HINDUISM IN CALCUTTA

Hinduism as a 'religion'

India's population includes followers of many religions and many people who have rejected religion in any form. The modern Republic of India has a secular constitution (one which guarantees the religious freedom of all but does not give a privileged position to any one religion) but a population which overwhelmingly identifies itself as Hindu. More than eighty per cent of India's population are Hindus, practitioners of what is now widely referred to as the religion of Hinduism. Historically, Hinduism has taken many different forms but has not organized itself around centralized authorities as have, for example, many Christian churches in Britain. Consequently, defining Hinduism as a 'religion' – its characteristics and boundaries – poses particular problems.

The term 'Hindu' was derived from the name of the river, now known as the Indus, that flows through the north-west of the Indian subcontinent. It was applied first to people living in the region around the Indus, and then to the inhabitants of the subcontinent of India as a whole. The English term 'Hinduism' was coined by Europeans (p.32). They used it to refer to the religion of the mass of the people who were neither Muslims nor followers of some other identifiable faith such as Buddhism or Sikhism.

EXERCISE

Knowing what you do about the origins of the term 'Hinduism', jot down any considerations you feel should govern our use of this term. Remember what you have discovered about the use of the term 'religion' and labels like 'Hinduism' in Section 4 (pp.31–8), and put into practice the critical approach outlined in Section 6. Be cautious before accepting labels and think about Hinduism in context.

DISCUSSION

You may well have suggested that the term 'Hinduism' should be used with care precisely because it is a *European* term which has been invented to categorize, or even 're-package', *Indian* assumptions and practices. Moreover, a label ending with an 'ism' can lead us to expect coherence and uniformity where there is none. Its use, especially when coupled with the term 'religion', may encourage the unthinking retention of European assumptions about what a religious system should look like. These are important considerations. They make us think more carefully about how we are to approach 'Hinduism', and about the adequacy of the concept of 'religion' as a tool for exploring different cultural contexts. It is indeed, therefore, a matter of looking at Indian Hinduism in its context. If you suggested that we should consult the opinion of Hindus before using these terms, this would seem to be a wise move. We shall do that now.

Many Hindus have adopted the conventional use of the terms 'Hinduism' and 'religion' while knowing that these do not translate underlying Hindu concepts. When you read John Bowker's brief account of Hinduism in Britain, you may have been surprised that one of the Hindus he interviewed declared that, 'Hinduism is not a religion, in the same sense in which Christianity is a religion, Islam is a religion and even Buddhism is a religion' (Bowker, 1983, p.27).

In 1944 Jawaharlal Nehru, who would soon be India's first post-independence prime minister, was one of many Indian leaders imprisoned by the British because of his support for the nationalist cause. Trapped in gaol, he had time to reflect on his Indian heritage. He was personally inclined towards secularism and, at times, was an outspoken critic of religion, but this did not prevent him from trying to understand its place in Indian society. This is what he had to say about the nature of Hinduism:

> Hinduism, as a faith, is vague, amorphous, many sided, all things to all men. It is hardly possible to define it, or indeed to say whether it is a religion or not, in the usual sense of the word.

> *(Nehru, 1960, p.63)*

Other Hindus have been well aware that the popular sense of the English term 'religion' ('its usual sense') conveys narrow and predominantly Christian overtones. Mohandas Karamchand Gandhi (1869–1948), the figurehead of the Hindu wing of the Indian independence movement who was given the title of 'Mahatma' ('the great soul'), preferred to speak of religion in its broadest sense, 'meaning thereby self-realization or knowledge of the self' (Gandhi, 1982, p.45). It is not enough, however, simply to adopt a definition of religion that is sufficiently broad to avoid being limited by the religious assumptions and norms of one culture. As we now know, a definition of religion must also be specific.

Some Hindus rely upon the concept of ***dharma***, in preference to the debated concept of 'religion', when explaining the nature of Hinduism. *Dharma* is a term taken from the ancient Indian language of Sanskrit in which many of Hinduism's sacred books were written. A limited number of Sanskrit terms will be introduced in the course of our discussion. Each term will be explained in the text and also, for quick reference, in the glossary.

> [*Dharma* can mean] 'religion', 'righteousness', 'duty', or 'innate nature'. According to Hinduism, man's innate nature is determined by a yearning for a restoration to its state of perfection. *Dharma* is the process by which the awareness of the realizable nature of perfection is enkindled in the heart of man.
>
> *(Mukerji, 1988, p.4)*

Within the Hindu tradition, the obligations of *dharma* fall under two broad headings: universal obligations and obligations specific to groups defined by age, sex and caste – a caste is a distinct social grouping with a traditional range of occupations that normally insists upon its members marrying within it. Caste has been a characteristic feature of Hindu life and social organization. Caste status is hereditary, and Hindu society has been organized historically around caste groups ranked in order of status according to traditional notions of ritual purity. Caste identity, therefore, indicates social status but also brings with it ritual responsibilities and social and economic implications. It also defines religious identity for, traditionally, only a person born to Hindu parents and thus into a caste has been counted as a Hindu. What we might wish to label as Hindu 'religious' activity, therefore, is inseparable from a complex socio-economic system in which family life and caste membership have their place.

One possibility open to us would be to identify as 'Hindu religion' or 'Hinduism' those beliefs and practices referred to by Hindus under the heading of *dharma*. But the central Hindu concept of *dharma*, although it can refer to social and ethical obligations and 'sacred law', embraces a view of life that does not distinguish between, for example, religion and politics, and religion and social custom in a manner commonly found in secular theories. If we begin with the Hindu concept of *dharma* and allow this to shape our understanding of the concept of 'Hinduism', we see that Hinduism refers to an entire way of life. Elements relating to 'sacred law' are all-pervasive and therefore not separable into a distinct compartment which we might label 'religion'.

Other religions allow us to turn to an authoritative prophet or founder-figure, or to a sacred book, to tell us exactly what that religion is about. Hinduism, however, brings together many different traditions and does not trace its beginnings back to one reputed founder or event. Hindu society is hierarchical, but Hinduism is not regulated by one centralized authority recognized by the majority of Hindus. Today it largely falls to India's *secular* courts to define the boundaries of Hinduism within the framework of the Indian Constitution. Harking back to 'Religion and social policy' (p.29), the definition of Hinduism as a religion has not been simply a matter of academic interest but has had far-reaching social and political implications for the Republic of India.

The diversity of Hinduism

The complex tradition now known as Hinduism has emerged largely from the coming together of four main elements:

1 The traditions of the original inhabitants of India, some of which may still continue in the cultures of India's more remote tribal peoples.

2 The influences of the Indus Valley civilization that flourished in north-west India until approximately the middle of the second millenium BCE.

3 The very old and highly developed culture inherited by the Tamil-speaking people of south India.

4 The religion brought into north-western India during the middle of the second millenium BCE by Indo-European settlers who called themselves '**aryans**' (*arya* or 'noble ones'). Their traditions have been perpetuated in the sacred text of the Veda (hence 'Vedic religion') and transmitted primarily by the **brahmin** caste, held to be the most ritually pure group in Hindu society and positioned at the top of the **hierarchy** of the Hindu caste structure.

(adapted from Klostermaier, 1989, p.31)

We know that the way in which religion is lived out by real people is often very different from the standards found in sacred books. Interviews on the streets of my local market would soon show that Christianity *as popularly practised* looks different from that found in the Bible and in creeds. I don't mean that people fail to live up to their beliefs (a different question), but simply that popular belief and practice rarely correspond to the 'official version' of any religion. 'Hinduism' certainly cannot be understood narrowly in terms of its most important sacred book, the Veda, and the practice of the caste entrusted with preserving it.

If you are beginning to despair about getting a clear picture of Hinduism, then you are on the right lines! This shows that you are beginning to get into the way of trying to see religion in context and not to make it conform to your expectations. For, as I explained earlier, the reason for taking Hinduism as an example in these units is because it will *not* be pressed into neat and tidy boxes. Thinking critically about the boundaries of Hinduism will help you to reflect further on the use of the concept 'religion' and the wider question of how to go about studying forms of religion.

EXERCISE

Hindus themselves are well aware that Hinduism tolerates a degree of variety that often confuses outsiders. This is how Sarvepalli Radhakrishnan (1888–1975), a notable Hindu philosopher and Indian statesman, summed up the differences within Hinduism:

In practical religion, Hinduism recognizes that there are those who wish to see God face to face, others who delight in the endeavour to know the truth of it all. Some find peace in action, others in non-action.

(Radhakrishnan, 1927, p.89)

I would like you now to consider these three questions:

1   What does this statement indicate about the nature of Hindu religious belief and practice?

2   What does it imply will be the likely outcome of concentrating upon just one form of Hindu belief and practice ?

3   Relating this statement about Hinduism to our ongoing concern with the way in which we study religion in general, to what extent, if at all, could Steve Bruce's definition of religion (p.37) and Ninian Smart's seven-dimensional model (p.36) cope with the differences that are all part of Hinduism?

DISCUSSION

1   Hinduism does not seem to require its followers to accept one view about the nature of ultimate reality. Some aim to 'see God face to face', which implies belief in a personal god. Others aim 'to know the truth of it all': a quest to realize the truth about the nature of reality that may not involve a commitment to a personal god. The distinction between preferences for 'action' and 'non-action' suggests that Hindus do not express their beliefs in one set form of practice.

2   It surely implies that concentrating on one form of Hindu belief and practice to the exclusion of the others would not do justice to the variety that is so characteristic of Hinduism.

3   Having tested Steve Bruce's definition of religion in Britain, I think we can now see that it could also cope with the variety of Hindu beliefs and practices. Remember, for example, his inclusion of supernatural entities and impersonal powers or processes. I think that this would embrace both those Hindus 'who wish to see God face to face' and those 'who delight in the endeavour to know the truth of it all'. Smart's seven-dimensional model is also sufficiently flexible to accommodate Hinduism, and taking each dimension in turn could provide a basis on which to bring together different examples of Hindu belief and practice. I will show you what I mean when we explore Hinduism in Calcutta.

Let's now relate Radhakrishnan's general statement about the 'practical religion' of Hinduism to the specific examples brought to life in TV15. Hindus often speak about their **ishtadeva** (chosen deity – I am going to use 'deity' to avoid the Christian overtones of God and because we will be talking about 'gods' and 'goddesses'). The *ishtadeva* of one Hindu may be the deity **Shiva** whereas another Hindu may revere **Kali**, the Mother Goddess (Figure 14/15.10). We might say that these Hindus wish to 'see God face to face'. In fact, Hindus speak of receiving the ***darshan*** (sight or vision) of their chosen deity, and the hope of receiving this provides a motive for going to a temple or maybe on pilgrimage. Yet, although many Hindus focus their devotions on a particular deity – for example, Kali – there has long been a tendency within Hinduism to view all the different deities as aspects of one supreme being. This vision of unity underlies the rich and varied religious symbolism that surrounds the actual practice of worship offered to many deities. Hindus typically become attached to one deity through family tradition or individual temperament rather than as a result of rejecting other deities. Devotion to an *ishtadeva* would not prevent respect being shown to other deities nor would it rule out participation in the rituals and festivals offered to them.

The path of worship and devotion is not of the same importance for all Hindus. Some Hindus speak of a non-personal reality, ***brahman*** (not to be confused with the caste), when explaining the nature of existence, and seek to experience a state of identity with this reality rather than a personal relationship with a deity. Worship and devotion are not rejected but are viewed as a starting point or aid to a more meditative path. This may lead some in time to a more solitary and ascetic lifestyle away from the ties of family and daily employment. Such people, I think, are those described by Radhakrishnan as endeavouring 'to know the truth of it all'.

Behind Radhakrishnan's reference to seeing God, knowing the truth of it all and paths of action and non-action is a well established distinction in Hinduism between the 'way of devotion' (worship), 'the way of wisdom' (meditation) and 'the way of action' (the responsibilities of ritual and *dharma*). All of these paths have value but none are obligatory. This helps to explain why, although temples may be thronged with devotees, Hindus will insist that nothing requires their attendance at temples. Attendance is merely one of a number of spiritually beneficial practices.

EXERCISE

This is a good point to pause and consolidate the background information provided so far about the broad features of Hinduism. Please read 'Introduction: Benares' in *Resource Book 3*, A6, which will give you an overview of Hinduism. Compare your impressions of the ancient city of Benares with the images of the modern city of Calcutta to be seen in TV15. ■

FIGURE 14/15.10 *Popular image of Kali. Photo: Sharma Picture Publications*

Worship in temples and street shrines

Apart from being intensely visible, participation in devotional practice at temples and festivals is extremely widespread within popular Hinduism. If we make allowance for regional and sectarian variations, we can gain some truly representative insights into a central preoccupation of living

Hinduism. As in Section 5, I would like you to look for examples of Smart's seven dimensions and again I will prompt you in the text from time to time.

If we are prepared to accept that expressions of reverence and respect for higher beings and powers are characteristics of 'religion', then signs of religion are not difficult to find in India. If you walked the streets of Calcutta as alertly as you walked the streets of Britain in our earlier exercise, you would see garlanded pictures and images of these higher beings and powers even on the dashboards of taxis and buses. The routine greeting of *namaskar*, when hands are raised with palms pressed together, is a gesture that has its place in Hindu worship. In the centre of cities as in the smallest villages, temples and shrines draw individuals into moments of intense contact with the chosen focus of their worship (*experiential and emotional dimension*). Conches, horns and cymbals are sounded in the larger temples. The evening air is alive with the scents and sounds of worship. It may seem as if religion is everywhere and that no one is apart from it.

A Hindu temple is a three-dimensional sacred space into which the devotee enters to receive the sight or vision (*darshan*) of the deity, for the purpose of the temple is to house the image (*murti*) of the deity (*material dimension*). The temple is the house of the deity and not the centre for congregational worship as found in some other religious traditions. Hindus generally go to a temple in India to fit in with the daily 'routine' of the deity and not on a special day in the week, unlike Hindus in Britain who now tend to concentrate their communal worship on Sundays simply for convenience. The main activity that takes place in a Hindu temple whether in India or Britain is worship (*puja*). It may take the form of an act of private devotion, a family ritual or a communal performance, and it has been described as 'the core ritual of popular theistic Hinduism' (Fuller, 1992, p.57). Thus *puja* can refer to an offering or prayer made by a solitary devotee or a complex ritual conducted on behalf of devotees by a temple attendant. It can even refer to the protracted worship that takes place during a festival over several days and thus means much the same as the English word 'festival'.

The symbolism of the divine encountered during the 'pilgrimage' of worship may include the aniconic (not shaped in human and animal form) in which the divine is represented, for example, by trees or stones shaped by nature alone. The divine is also portrayed in immensely varied human and animal figures. **Ganesh**, one of the most popular Hindu deities, is depicted as pot-bellied with the head of an elephant (Figure 14/15.11). According to Hindu mythology, Ganesh is the son of Shiva and dramatic stories are told about how he came to have the head of an elephant at the hands of his divine father. By way of compensation, Shiva made Ganesh the remover of obstacles and the maker of auspicious occasions. For this reason, Ganesh is frequently worshipped at the start of *puja* or when undertaking any important or momentous activity. Shrines to Ganesh are often found just within the entrance to a temple compound.

FIGURE 14/15.11   *Popular image of Ganesh. Photo: Sharma Picture Publications*

Wayside shrines and household shrines serve much the same purpose as the temple (Figure 14/15.12). All of them are inclusive in their acceptance of these varied symbols of the divine (see the TV15 sequence on the Armenian Ghat). In dealing with forms of belief and practice that are so varied and yet all have their place within Hinduism, you are probably beginning to apply instinctively the broad principles of Religious Studies: namely, trying to understand what lies before you on its own terms and in context.

FIGURE 14/15.12   *Street shrine of Shiva, Gol Park, Calcutta. Photo: Gwilym Beckerlegge*

Now that you have some understanding of the characteristic patterns of Hindu worship, we shall take a closer look at examples of living Hinduism in eastern India and more particularly in the city of Calcutta in the state of West Bengal.

Hinduism in eastern India: religion in Calcutta

The Hinduism of Bengal, as in other regions of India with their own languages and distinctive historical traditions, has absorbed and retained many local elements which make it peculiarly the Hinduism of Bengal. The city of Calcutta has exerted its own considerable influence upon the surrounding region. Calcutta, the capital of West Bengal, was founded in 1690 originally as a British trading post on the Hugli, a stretch of the Ganges (or Ganga), a river sacred to Hindus (see Figure 14/15.13).

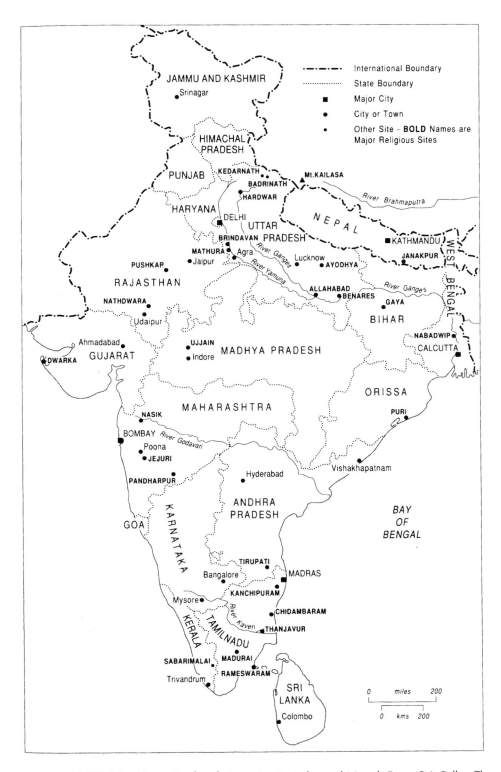

FIGURE 14/15.13   *Major Hindu religious sites in India and Nepal. From C.J. Fuller,* The Camphor Flame, *p.xvii. Copyright c.1992 by Princeton University Press, reprinted by permission of Princeton University Press*

During the following century, Calcutta became the administrative capital of the British Presidency of Bengal and in 1858 became the capital of British India, a status it was to lose to New Delhi once Indian nationalism intensified in Bengal during the first decade of the twentieth century. Calcutta, therefore, is not an ancient Hindu city like Benares (or Varanasi), which developed partly as a centre of pilgrimage.

Calcutta began life and continues as a cosmopolitan trading city. It is home to a substantial Muslim population and followers of other religions. It thrives as an artistic centre for writers and film-makers. The name of the city, however, harks back to its antecedents. 'Calcutta' is believed to come either from the name of an earlier village absorbed by the growth of the city or from 'Kalikshetra', meaning the 'field' or place of the Mother Goddess, Kali. This is an allusion to the temple of Kalighat which existed prior to the growth of the city, although on a different site, and continues as a place of pilgrimage in Calcutta today. Kali (The 'Dark One') is another form of the Mother Goddess (or *devi*) who is frequently depicted in Hindu myths as the consort of Shiva, one of the most widely known and worshipped Hindu deities. The Mother Goddess is also worshipped under the name of **Durga** (The 'Unfathomable One') in Bengal and particularly during the great festival of Durga Puja in Calcutta.

As a centre of traditional Kali worship, Calcutta draws pilgrims to its temples and festivals dedicated to the Mother Goddess. Temples and other religious sites in Calcutta on the banks of or close to the Hugli are particularly likely to attract pilgrims. Contact with British and European thought during the time of British rule and the city's role as a cosmopolitan centre have also made it open to foreign ideas. The openness of Calcutta to novel and alien ideas has challenged Hindu intellectuals from the city to lead the way in shaping Hindu responses to new ideas, as we will discover later when we consider Hinduism as a 'world religion' (*doctrinal and philosophical dimension*). If you look at the map in Figure 14/15.13, you will see that Calcutta dominates the north-eastern quarter of India. As a state capital and commercial centre, Calcutta pulls many workers from India's professional and administrative élite. The city has also acted as a magnet to the poor, who have been drawn by the allure of finding new opportunities. Many of these migrants have brought with them their own styles of Hinduism and have added to the variety already found within Bengal.

TV15 illustrates something of the variety of deities worshipped under the umbrella of 'Hinduism' in this city. The most obvious starting point is the worship of Kali in two of Calcutta's most well-known temples, Kalighat and Dakshineswar. Here devotees also pay their respects to other deities, like **Krishna**, who are housed in the same temple compound. I want you now to follow a worshipper on a 'pilgrimage in miniature' around Dakshineswar temple on the outskirts of Calcutta. Before you read further, please study carefully the plan of Dakshineswar temple in Figure 14/15.14. There are sequences showing this temple in TV15.

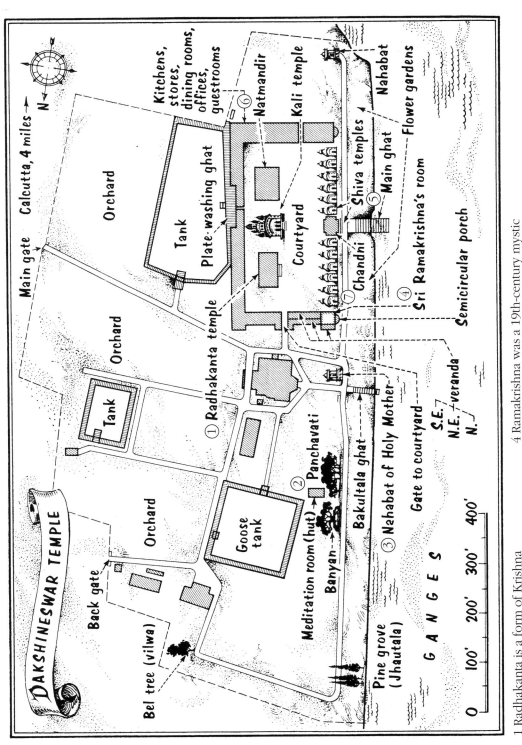

FIGURE 14/15.14 *Plan of Dakshineswar temple. From Christopher Isherwood, Ramakrishna and his Disciples, 1965, Methuen, p.216. Reproduced by permission of the Vedanta Society of Southern California*

1 Radhakanta is a form of Krishna
2 Panchavati is a meditation grove
3 Nahabat is a music house. The Holy Mother was the wife of Ramakrishna
4 Ramakrishna was a 19th-century mystic
5 Ghat is an acess point to water in a river or pond
6 Natmandir is a covered area for dance, music, drama and debate
7 Chandni is a portico

Dakshineswar temple is ringed by a number of tanks and **ghats** (steps or platforms) that provide access to water. Bathing plays an important part in the preparations for Hindu worship because, in washing themselves, the devotees achieve not just a state of physical cleanliness but also undergo a purification before participating in the rituals of worship (*practical and ritual dimension*). For some, a ritual bathe at the temple would precede worship. Having bought flowers from the stalls outside, devotees leave their shoes (closely guarded) at the entrance as they enter the main temple compound. This is a large flagged area flanked by small temples in honour of different deities but overlooked by the imposing temple of Kali, the deity to whom the whole complex is dedicated (the 'presiding deity'). It would be natural for worship to be offered here first of all. Beneath the mass of the Kali temple lies the 'womb-room' – the small inmost chamber where the image of the deity resides. Devotees make offerings of flowers and coins at the door and in the sight of the image but do not go inside. This is where the difference between Hindu temple worship and the types of 'congregational' worship commonly found in Britain, for example, begins to hit you. You have to set aside assumptions about 'congregational' worship, if this is what you know best, in order to understand what goes on in a Hindu temple. Think of Kali holding court. At certain times of the day, there is a public audience when the priests act like courtiers and present the offerings that devotees bring to the goddess.

To walk around the Kali temple is part of the 'pilgrimage'. The compound also contains temples to Shiva, the consort of Kali, and to Krishna who with his consort, **Radha**, is worshipped the length and breadth of India. The devotees go to each in turn. Before they leave they also pay their respects in the room set aside in memory of Ramakrishna, a popular Hindu teacher who was a temple attendant at Dakshineswar in the last century. Hindu temples often provide doles of food for the poor so, on leaving the temple, worshippers might make a donation for this purpose or give alms to the needy who often gather around popular temples (*ethical and legal dimension*).

Many of the migrants to Calcutta adopt the worship of Kali, the Mother Goddess, because it is so widespread in Bengal, but others 'bring their gods with them'. TV15 shows workers from the nearby Indian state of Orissa now living in the heart of the city on and around the Armenian Ghat on the banks of the Hugli. The Orissans living at the Ghat have erected a shrine dedicated to Lord **Jagannatha**, a name given to the deity **Vishnu** symbolized in a highly distinctive form that is particularly associated with the Jagannatha temple in the city of Puri, Orissa (Figure 14/15.15). Vishnu is worshipped throughout India but is commonly addressed either by the names found in accounts of his appearances on earth, such as Krishna, or by titles such as Jagannatha (meaning 'Lord of the World').

FIGURE 14/15.15   *Popular image of Jagannath (right-hand figure). Photo: L. Dhawan Brothers, Gaya*

Although Hindus in Calcutta may originally have come from different parts of India and have brought their own styles of Hinduism with them, this will not prevent them from sharing wholeheartedly in the great religious festival that Calcutta has made its own – Durga Puja, the worship of the Mother Goddess. This festival takes over the life of the city and indeed comes close to stopping the traffic at the end of the rainy season.

The festival of Durga Puja in Calcutta

Although Hindus are not required to attend temples on set days in the week, the Hindu year is punctuated by days dictated by the lunar calendar during which *puja* (worship) should be offered to a particular deity or deities. Hindu festivals often combine the marking of the changing of the seasons and the honouring of deities. The emphasis given to specific festivals and to aspects of the same festival will vary from region to region. Individuals attend festivals for many reasons: to honour the deity, as an opportunity to seek guidance and practical help from the deity, to share in what is after all a performance, and to be part of a family and community gathering.

In a temple-based festival or one held to honour a deity revered as the protector of the town or village, the climax of the festival is likely to be a public procession bearing the *murti* (image) of the deity through the streets. The reason for moving the deity will vary according to local myths and legends (*narrative or mythic dimension*). If the festival is not temple-based but still centres upon *puja*, celebrations begin when preparations are made to receive and install the *murti* of the appropriate deity in the home or on the street. Communal worship is by no means confined to temples. For some time prior to the festival, local craftsmen will have devoted considerable time to the manufacture of the *murti* of the deity or deities to be honoured (Figure 14/15.16). These craftsmen normally belong to particular castes and are likely to live and work in close proximity to one another. Much of their livelihood for the year may

FIGURE 14/15.16 *Urban craftsman painting image of a deity, Gol Park, Calcutta. Photo: Gwilym Beckerlegge*

depend upon supplying the *murti* necessary to celebrate the most popular festival in their region. Nowadays, many of these craftsmen also service the tourist industry. There can't be many tourists who have visited India and not come away with an image of a Hindu deity. Hindus who wish to purchase a *murti* often collaborate in family, caste, occupational and neighbourhood groups to buy a suitable image. The collaborative purchase of festival *murti* is an opportunity for competition between groups determined to display the most elaborate image and build the best decorated **pandal**, the platform which bears and screens the image of the deity (*social and institutional dimension*).

During the course of the festival, *puja* is offered to the appropriate deities, and there may be rituals carried out separately according to the age and sex of the participants. At the end of the festival, the *murti* is carried in a carnival-like procession through the streets before being returned to the water from where the clay out of which it was made was taken. The celebration is likely to involve some serious music-making, the throwing of coloured powder over friends and passers-by for good luck, and dancing by men and boys. The side of a village pond, the seashore or the banks of one of India's great rivers is the place from which the celebrants return home and so to everyday life.

Durga Puja is one name for a festival that is celebrated under different names, **Navratri** and **Dasshera** being the most common, and with different shades of meaning across India. In contemporary India popular festivals are often marked by state holidays. In Bengal the great festival of Durga Puja, which falls at the end of the monsoon season, is one such occasion for a vast public celebration. Although some families in the city take advantage of the festival holiday in order to visit family homes in the countryside, for many it would be unthinkable to leave Calcutta and miss the vast, public celebration of this festival. The growth of urban centres like Calcutta has provided new arenas for public worship, and has stimulated the traditional crafts involved in supplying the images and other materials necessary for the celebration of the festival.

EXERCISE

Please read the account of 'Durga Puja in Calcutta' by Jaya Chaliha and Bunny Gupta in the *Resource Book 3*, A7. It refers to locations in Calcutta that are likely to be unfamiliar to you, but you will find that most of the references to Bengali Hindu culture are explained. Use the reading to get some sense and feel of the occasion of the festival. Then from this account of Durga Puja and from these units, identify examples of the way in which the celebration of Durga Puja defies being placed in one separate category that might be labelled 'religion'. (The festival is also described in TV15 and the related *Audio-visual Notes*.)

DISCUSSION

The festival has been transformed from being a festival in honour of Durga, which originally was celebrated privately within the confines of a few wealthy families, to being a popular festival of the masses widely celebrated as a public holiday. In the process Durga Puja has picked up overtones and elements that have as little to do with its original form, as has Father Christmas with the Christian celebration of Christmas, but which would now be equally difficult to dislodge. It is a heavily commercialized event with shops advertising their Durga Puja sales (Figures 14/15.17 and 18), and its celebration draws in both Indian popular music and Indian cinema. The festival has been a vehicle for the expression of nationalist and other political sentiments and for many is a symbol of their citizenship of Calcutta. The construction of *pandals* and the purchase of *murti* are very much linked with community pride and status. The festival thus illustrates the workings of the Hindu social system. This is evident in the roles performed by those who organize the celebration of the festival and the functions performed by castes whose traditional livelihoods are partly dependent upon preparing for the festival and carrying out the necessary rituals. Commerce, politics, citizenship are as much a part of Durga Puja as is worship of the Mother Goddess, Durga.

Our brief exposure to Hinduism in Calcutta has revealed a number of things about the nature of Hinduism that have implications for the use of the term 'religion'. Working with the title of Hinduism and accepting it as a 'religion', we have discovered a tradition whose followers are created by birth. Membership of Hinduism, the 'religion', and of Hindu society are one and the same. We have also seen that the artificial mould of 'Hinduism' contains such a variety of beliefs and practices that it makes defining Hinduism in terms of universally accepted beliefs and practices virtually impossible. Even the most visible and popular practices and beliefs tied to *puja* are immensely varied, directed to different deities, and are not common to all Hindus. For some Hindus, however, their sense of living in a world of many 'religions' has led them to set out the principles of Hinduism in a more systematic way.

FIGURE 14/15.17   *Wishing you a happier, healthier and cleaner Pooja – advertisement for Eureka Forbes Ltd in* The Statesman *(Calcutta) Thursday 28 September 1995. Reproduced by permission of Eureka Forbes Ltd*

FIGURE 14/15.18   *This Durga Puja, celebrate a sound victory – advertisement for BPL Technologies Ltd in* The Telegraph *(Calcutta) Tuesday 3 October 1995. Reproduced by permission of the BPL Group, India*

Hinduism as 'a world religion': a more recent understanding

Traditionally, as we have seen, a Hindu was someone born to Hindu parents and into a caste with its appropriate *dharma*. The link between religious practice and a whole way of life bound the individual into a community from birth. Regional factors, parentage and caste affiliation largely determined the particular style of religious belief and practice adopted by individual Hindus. It has proved difficult, because of this, for individuals to detach a religious dimension that could be changed without sacrificing membership of their community. The assumption that birth provides the entry point into a religious identity is by no means confined to Hinduism. Orthodox Jewish identity, for example, is generally established through the mother. Although Orthodox Jewish communities admit converts, Orthodox Jews historically have not set out to seek them, unlike, for example, Christianity and Islam.

During the last two centuries, some Hindu thinkers have developed a rather different understanding of the Hindu tradition. They have encouraged its redefinition not just as 'a religion' but as a 'world religion' and as something distinct from Hindu culture in its broadest sense. During the nineteenth century several prominent Hindu religious leaders and intellectuals travelled to the West, where they defended their religious heritage in response to criticisms by Christian missionaries. They were also able to talk about the nature of Hinduism with interested audiences. These Hindus, largely from Bengal and exposed to Western influence in Calcutta, found that 'What is Hinduism?' was a question that non-Hindu audiences wanted to have answered in a way that would be intelligible in terms of Western, and thus largely Christian, notions of 'religion'.

It has been claimed that it was Swami Vivekananda, a nineteenth-century Bengali religious teacher, who presented 'Hinduism for the first time to the world as a universal faith' and so 'raised Hinduism to the status of a world religion in the outside world' (Weightman, 1984, p.231). Vivekananda (*svamin* or **Swami** is a religious title) was responsible for creating an organization called the Ramakrishna Math and Mission. Ramakrishna was Vivekananda's spiritual teacher and, you may remember, the temple at Dakshineswar is visited by worshippers today partly because Ramakrishna spent much of his life there (p.68). The Ramakrishna Math and Mission is committed to the promotion of practical service to humanity and a philosophy of a universal religion. The Math is its monastic wing and the Mission is made up of lay supporters. The Movement today has more than 120 branches world-wide, including one in Britain, although the greatest number are to be found in India. Its headquarters, Belur Math, established in 1898, lies across the Ganges from the city of Calcutta and is featured in TV15.

Vivekananda recognized the seeds of a universal religion in all religions but believed that the signs of this were most apparent in certain strands within Hinduism. The impact of presenting Hinduism in this way is evident today. It comes through in the way in which British Hindus interviewed by John Bowker speak of 'all religions blending into one' and of the same basic elements in all religions (see *Resource Book 3*, A3).

The architectural style and the symbolism from a number of religions have been incorporated into the design of the temple at Belur Math, the headquarters of the Ramakrishna Math and Mission, as a way of conveying the 'universal faith' in which the movement believes. This is a prime example of the importance of the *material dimension* of religion. We can 'read' quite a lot from the brief shot of the outside of this temple in TV15. The main entrance of the temple, which was dedicated in 1938, has a façade influenced by Buddhist architectural style. The structure which rises over the entrance is modelled on the Hindu temples of south India with their lofty towers. The windows and balconies inside the temple draw upon the Rajput (Hindu) and Mughal (Islamic) styles of north India. The central dome is derived from European architecture of the Renaissance period, while the ground plan of the interior gives the impression of a Christian cross. The differences between Belur Math and the more typical Hindu temples at Kalighat and Dakshineswar can be seen in the comparative sequences in TV15. The differences in their design and the symbols they use are deliberate and tell us a lot about what kind of Hinduism they represent.

Vivekananda spent four years in the United States and Western Europe touring and lecturing. By the time he created the Ramakrishna Math and Mission on his return to India in 1897, his message had already been widely heard. Most of those who heard him speak were not Hindus by birth, but many were dissatisfied with the Christianity of the churches. They still clung to the hope of finding a religion that would satisfy them. During two visits to the West before his death in 1902, Vivekananda founded a number of societies dedicated to the study of Hindu religious philosophy, and accepted Americans and Europeans into both the lay and monastic wings of the Ramakrishna Math and Mission. From this time on, at least certain aspects of Hinduism would no longer be open only to those born as Hindus and into membership of a caste.

The growth in the number of Hindu groups that define their 'membership' very differently from earlier Hindu notions of a way of life resulting from birth into a caste has been a feature of the development of Hinduism during the last century. The Ramakrishna Math and Mission is one Hindu group with this wider 'membership'. Another internationally known example is the International Society for Krishna Consciousness (ISKCON – popularly known as the 'Hare Krishnas'), which has adopted a more active missionary strategy in the attempt to make converts from those not born into Hindu families. ISKCON has been active in Britain since the late 1960s. Its members, sometimes dressed in saffron robes, might have approached you on the streets. Whether the 'converts' gathered by such movements can really be counted as Hindus has been questioned both by other Hindus outside these organizations and by some scholars who continue to emphasize the earlier notion of Hindu identity being conferred through birth.

Having to explain the nature of their beliefs on a world stage has unquestionably affected the way in which many prominent Hindu teachers and scholars have defined their understanding of Hinduism. This relatively recent way of explaining Hinduism shows an awareness of what the English-speaking world understands by 'religion' and a tendency to explain Hinduism in these terms. This has become more pronounced in the writings of many twentieth-century Hindu thinkers and Indian philosophers, in the way in which practising Hindus talk about their beliefs, and in the novel acceptance of an expanded global 'membership' by certain Hindu groups. These tendencies should not overshadow the greater part of the vibrant, living Hindu tradition which lacks such clearly defined boundaries.

8 THE TERM 'RELIGION': A CONCLUDING COMMENT

I hope that this more extended study of religion in context has been interesting in itself and that you have glimpsed something of the richness of Hinduism. We have made this brief study of Hinduism also to put to work some of the principles in the study of religion that we met earlier in these units. I want finally to draw some threads together by considering more generally the problems and pitfalls of using the concept of 'religion' in a cross-cultural study.

Applying what we had discovered in Section 4 about the term 'religion', we tried to avoid plunging into our study of Hinduism assuming that we knew what a 'religion' should look like. We began by noting that the concept of 'Hinduism' is a European invention and that its use creates its own complications. Turning to what Hindus say about their own beliefs, we found that some Hindu thinkers have identified the Sanskrit concept of *dharma* as one sharing the general sense of the English use of 'religion'. These thinkers have maintained, however, that *dharma*, due to its social and moral overtones, is the broader concept. This understanding of *dharma* would appear to imply that 'religion' is not a distinct compartment in the total package of an individual's beliefs and practices. We heard some Hindus say that Hinduism is not so much a 'religion' as 'a way of life'.

We need to look more closely at the distinction between 'religion' and 'way of life' because few people who identify themselves as religious would be satisfied with the suggestion that religion was anything less than a whole way of life. A Muslim in TV14, speaking from the perspective of a faith very different from Hinduism, also rejected the label 'religion' as a satisfactory way of explaining the nature of Islam. He referred instead to the Arabic *din*, a 'way of life'. No doubt Christians would also reject any suggestion that their religion was less than a 'way of life'.

In drawing their distinctions between 'religion' and 'way of life', it is possible that those who reject 'religion' in favour of 'way of life' have in mind the manner in which religion in Europe (and in other parts of the world, for that matter) has become increasingly a matter of private belief and morality seen most obviously and distinctively in the public sphere only on set occasions. I think we would recognize this as an accurate description of the place of religion in mainstream, contemporary British society. When addressing Western audiences, Hindu thinkers who have spoken of Hinduism as a 'way of life' rather than as a 'religion' may also have in mind the Christian emphasis upon 'right belief' – orthodoxy – and the resulting tendency to see religion as a matter of belief. Even from our limited survey of Hinduism and its rich variety, we can appreciate that what has come to be known as Hinduism is characterized not by 'orthodoxy' in the details of belief, but rather by broadly shared assumptions and practices bound together in a distinctive social organization.

Given the new notions that became progressively attached to the terms 'religion' and 'the religions' in European thought from the eighteenth century onwards (pp.32–3), we can push our analysis of the problems encountered when using these terms a stage further. These new notions, you will remember, were themselves shaped under the influence of rationalist and secularizing tendencies. It is, therefore, hardly surprising that we meet particular problems when applying these terms in cultural contexts where what we seek to define as 'religion' runs through all aspects of life and through social organizations and institutions, rather than standing apart as a separate, visible element as religion tends to do in surroundings that are more generally secular. It is true that India has a secular constitution but, to date, the obligations of Hindu *dharma* continue to be discharged on a daily basis by millions of individuals in all aspects of their lives – for example, in the way in which they wash and in their occupations.

So, should we abandon the term 'religion'? I would not draw this conclusion, partly because this would probably signal the hunt for a concept to replace 'religion' which would lead us back to exactly the same problems. Terms like 'faith', 'tradition', 'worldview', 'meaning-system', 'moral community' and 'symbolic community' are all to be found in scholarly writing, but it is difficult to see how these will help us any better to achieve the right balance between being specific and yet flexible when dealing with different cultural contexts. As I tried to show you when we looked at Hindu worship, I think what we need to do is to find definitions and models of 'religion' that can pass the test of working in the study of different cultures. So, I would say, let's keep the term 'religion', but make sure that we use it with care and with particular sensitivity when studying societies that have not had a hand in shaping the definition of this peculiarly European concept. If you disagree with this conclusion, you might like to make out a case for using a different concept. You now have a grounding in the skills and knowledge you will need to do that – to do Religious Studies.

This is the point when you might like to look again at the objectives listed at the beginning of these units. You will return to the study of religion in A103 when you come to Block 6. There you will look more specifically at 'new religious movements'. The knowledge you now have of the major features of some of the longer-established religions and of the methods of Religious Studies will help you when you consider these new and often controversial religious movements. The remaining two units of this block, however, will introduce you to the History of Science. In spite of the way in which religion and science have often been portrayed as being at loggerheads, I think you will find that the methods of these two disciplines share a number of common features.

GLOSSARY

Allah Muslim name for the one God; not a personal name, having the sense of 'the God'.

aryan 'noble' or 'pure'. Used of themselves and their traditions by Indo-Europeans who migrated into ancient India and whose beliefs are preserved in early parts of the Veda.

autonomous following its own laws; when applied to religion, this implies that religion is an entirely distinctive phenomenon and thus can only be understood on its own terms. The Latin phrase *sui generis* (of its own kind) is sometimes used to make this point.

Bhagavad Gita 'Song of the Lord': a Hindu religious text.

Bible usually refers to Christian scriptures comprising both the Old and New Testaments.

brahman ultimate power or reality underlying the visible world.

brahmin 'priestly' class in the Hindu social system.

church place where Christians meet for worship but also the world-wide community of Christians, or a particular community of Christians.

darshan 'sight' or vision of the deity. In these units *darshan* refers to standing in the presence of the sacred in the expectation that the 'sight' of the deity will bring a blessing.

Dasshera one name given to the string of Hindu festivals that fall at the end of the monsoon season. The first nine nights are also known as Navratri and, in Bengal, Durga Puja is celebrated during this time.

deva (m) and *devi* (f) 'shining one' meaning respectively 'god' and 'goddess' in Hinduism.

dharma right conduct, duty, way of life.

dianetics therapeutic system devised by L. Ron Hubbard, the founder of Scientology.

Durga 'unfathomable one'; one of the names given to the Mother Goddess in Hinduism, the consort of Shiva and the embodiment of his energy.

engrams used in the theory of Scientology to refer to the imprints of past traumatic experiences upon the embodied spirit of the human being.

Five Ks from five Punjabi words beginning with 'k' that refer to the five symbols adopted by devout Sikhs: uncut hair, wearing a comb to bind the hair, a steel bangle, an ornamental dagger, and loose shorts usually worn as undergarments.

Ganesh Hindu deity known as the remover of obstacles and maker of auspicious occasions.

ghat steps leading to water, or a landing place by a river where Hindus perform rituals.

gurdwara 'door to the guru', a Sikh temple.

guru spiritual teacher, the term is found in both the Hindu and Sikh traditions.

hierarchy graded social order but may refer more specifically to a religious order made up of ranks.

ideology system of beliefs, and more particularly a system of beliefs which influences the kinds of behaviour approved of and disapproved of by a group. In a political context, the system of beliefs that shapes the policy of a party. This term has further technical meanings as, for example, in Marxism.

imam Muslim prayer leader.

ishtadeva chosen deity of an individual Hindu.

Jagannatha 'Lord of the World'; title given to the Hindu deity Vishnu, particularly to that form of the god worshipped at the great temple of that name in the city of Puri.

Kali 'dark one': a popular name given to the Mother Goddess, in Hinduism the consort of Shiva and the embodiment of his energy.

kosher 'right' food; food prepared according to Jewish law.

Krishna name of one of the earthly forms taken by the Hindu deity Vishnu who is believed by his devotees to have manifested himself to preserve righteousness when threatened by demonic powers. Krishna is a very popular Hindu deity.

Messiah 'anointed one' expected by Jews to inaugurate an age of universal peace when, among other things, exiled Jews will be restored to the Holy Land.

mihrab niche in the wall of a Muslim mosque indicating the direction of Mecca.

moksha 'liberation': the achievement of spiritual perfection and thus release from repeated rebirths according to Hindu religious belief.

mosque 'place of prostration'; a Muslim place of prayer.

murti 'embodiment', image (of a Hindu deity).

namaskar Hindu greeting in the spirit of worship.

Navratri see **Dasshera**.

pandal platform, usually ornate, upon which the image of a Hindu deity is placed.

Protestants Christians following reformers who rejected the authority of the Pope together with much Roman Catholic theology.

puja Hindu worship.

Qur'an sacred scripture of Islam.

rabbi Jewish scholar learned in Torah and qualified to make judgements on points of Jewish belief, practice and law.

Radha name of Krishna's consort, often depicted with him in religious iconography.

Radhakanta literally, 'Radha's lover' – another title for Krishna.

Roman Catholic largest church of Western Christianity under the authority of the Pope.

secularization process by which religious institutions lose their social significance.

Shabbat Jewish sabbath beginning at dusk on Friday nights.

Shiva Hindu deity associated with time, the destruction of the cosmic cycle and meditation.

siddhi 'achievement', supernatural powers believed by Hindus to be acquired through skill in meditation techniques and other means.

Swami 'Lord', title given to a Hindu holy man roughly equivalent to the English use of 'reverend'.

synagogue 'place of gathering'; Jewish place of worship where Torah is expounded.

thetans reincarnated, embodied spirits trapped in human beings according to the theory of Scientology.

Torah 'teaching', Jewish sacred law and instruction.

Veda 'knowledge', but used more generally to refer to the Veda – authoritative scriptures believed by Hindus to have been revealed originally to ancient seers.

Vishnu Hindu deity associated with the sun and regarded as the sustainer of the cosmic cycle.

REFERENCES

BAIRD, R (1982) 'Religious or non-religious: TM in American courts', *Journal of Dharma*, vol.7, no.4, pp.391–407.

BARKER, E. (1989) *New Religious Movements – A Practical Introduction*, London, HMSO.

BECKFORD, J.A. (1985) *Cult Controversies: The Societal Response to New Religious Movements*, London, Tavistock.

BOWKER, J. (1983) *Worlds of Faith*, London, Ariel Books, BBC.

BRUCE, S. (1995) *Religion in Modern Britain*, Oxford University Press.

CHAUDHURI, S. (ed.) (1990) *Calcutta: The Living City*, Oxford University Press.

DENISTON, D. and MCWILLIAMS, P. (1975) *The TM Book – How to Enjoy the Rest of Your Life*, Los Angeles, Price/Stern/Sloan.

FULLER, C.J. (1992) *The Camphor Flame*, Princeton University Press.

GANDHI, M.K. (1982) *An Autobiography or The Story of My Experiments with Truth*, Harmondsworth, Penguin.

HAMILTON, M.B. (1995) *The Sociology of Religion*, London, Routledge.

ISHERWOOD, C. (1986) *Ramakrishna and His Disciples*, London, Shepheard-Walwyn.

KINSLEY, D.R. (1982) *Hinduism*, Eaglewood Cliffs, NJ, Prentice-Hall.

KLOSTERMAIER, K. (1989) *A Survey of Hinduism*, State University of New York Press.

MUKERJI, B. (1988) *The Hindu Tradition*, New York, Amity House.

NEHRU, J. (1960) *The Discovery of India*, London, Meridian Books.

OTTO, R. (1970, 2nd edn) *The Idea of the Holy*, Oxford University Press first published 1958.

RADHAKRISHNAN, S. (1964, 13th imp.) *The Hindu View of Life*, London, George Allen and Unwin, first published 1927.

SMART, N. (1989) *The World's Religions: Old Traditions and Modern Transformations*, Cambridge University Press.

SMITH, W.C. (1963) *The Meaning and End of Religion*, New York, The Macmillan Company.

THOMAS, T. (ed.) (1988) *The British: Their Religious Beliefs and Practices 1800–1986*, London, Routledge.

WEIGHTMAN, S. (1984) 'Hinduism' in J.R. Hinnells (ed.) *A Handbook of Living Religions*, Harmondsworth, Penguin.

YINGER, J.M. (1970) *The Scientific Study of Religion*, London, Macmillan.

UNITS 16 AND 17 HERE'S HISTORY OF SCIENCE

Written for the course team by James Moore

Contents

STUDY WEEKS SIXTEEN & SEVENTEEN

STUDY COMPONENTS				
Weeks of study	Texts	TV	AC	Set books
2	*Resource Book 3* *Illustration Book*	TV16 TV17	–	–

Aims and objectives

These units aim to establish the following criteria for studying the history of science:

1   that 'science' has a history – its meaning has changed through time;

2   that the knowledge-content of science – our understanding of nature – is the contingent product of natural human activities, with no guarantee of progressively better interpretations;

3   that what comes to be seen as true in science is to be explained historically in the same way as, or symmetrically with, what comes to be seen as false.

4   that History of Science as a discipline specializes in such explanations. The resources on which it draws are to be seen as 'contextual' rather than 'internal' or 'external' to the science of any period.

Your objectives in studying these units should be:

1   to understand and be able to explain each of the criteria above;

2   to illustrate these criteria from, and apply them to, the career of the Victorian naturalist Alfred Russel Wallace (1823–1913).

1 MEET MR WALLACE

Late in 1912 a tall, white-haired pensioner sat alone in his study overlooking Poole Harbour in Dorset. He was elderly and almost housebound but his senses were keen and his faculties razor-sharp. He hunched over his desk, writing in a bold, rounded hand. This was to be his literary last will and testament; he had a lifetime's conviction to pass on: his profound belief in the equality of intellect and moral character among human beings, past and present.

Not a popular view this, least of all among Englishmen who studied the religions of India. So the old man picked up a translation of the ancient Hindu scriptures, the Vedas, and copied out long passages. Here, he noted, was a 'vast system of religious teaching as pure and lofty as those

FIGURE 16/17.1   *Alfred Russel Wallace in 1913, age 90. From J. Marchant,* Alfred Russel Wallace, *1916, London, Cassell, vol.2, frontispiece*

of the finest portions of the Hebrew scriptures', the Old Testament. Allowing for 'the very limited knowledge of Nature at this early period', the various writers were 'fully our equals in their conceptions of the universe, and of the Deity'. Their minds 'could not have been in any way inferior to those of the best of our religious teachers and poets – to our Miltons and our Tennysons'.

The old man loved flouting convention. His pen pranced on, twitting every toff brought up on the classics. The civilization of ancient India, which gave the world the Vedas, was the intellectual 'equal ... of early classical races, in grand temples, forts and palaces, weapons and implements, jewelry and exquisite fabrics'. Owing to a tropical climate, its surviving architecture may be less ancient than that of Greece or Rome, but – now he poked at parsons – buildings 'corresponding in age to the period of our Gothic cathedrals are immensely numerous, and show an originality of design, a wealth of ornament, and a perfection of workmanship equal to those of any other buildings in the world'.

More blithe iconoclasm, of course. The 'great majority of educated persons' hold that we are 'really more intellectual and wiser than the men of past ages – that our mental faculties have increased in power'. This was a shibboleth of the last century but, the old man snorted, 'the idea is totally unfounded'. 'We are the inheritors of the accumulated knowledge of all the ages.' And who knows? Perhaps the 'first steps taken in the accumulation of this vast mental treasury required even more thought and a higher intellectual power than any of those taken in our own era' (Wallace, 1913, pp.11, 14–15, 25).

There spoke one who had left school at fourteen to become one of the nineteenth century's most noted and controversial scientists. He backed minorities, fringe movements, even heresies. He tangled with as much as he typified in his time, and his death at ninety a year later, on the eve of World War I, marks the end of the Victorian era. Never again would a self-made scientist pronounce on so much, so vociferously, and so obstinately for so long. This is one reason why Alfred Russel Wallace remains interesting and important. It is also why he offers an excellent entrée to History of Science.

'Alfred Russel who? Marconi gave us the wireless, Edison the electric light. Darwin put apes in our family tree and Pasteur launched long-life milk. But who was Wallace? What did he do for posterity? Why waste time studying a nobody – an oddball to boot – with so many greats to choose from?'

You may well ask.

'And anyway, isn't this course about the humanities? History was weeks ago – primary sources and all that. We did have art *history at the start, but then painting and architecture are what we signed up for, not science. Science is about abstruse theories and obscure experiments. Why ask us to study such things? There must be some mistake.'*

If any of these questions have occurred to you, you are already well into History of Science. They are the very questions the discipline has to answer when accounting for its existence. Its subjects and methods need explaining; its history must be related to history as studied elsewhere in the humanities. So before looking closer at Wallace's life and scientific career, let's tackle the underlying questions.

2 GETTING STARTED

No trespassing?

The first and most obvious historical point to make is that scientists and humanities people have had a lot to say about one another's work. You've seen evidence of this already.

EXERCISE

Look over the first four paragraphs above and note down the humanities disciplines (as found in this course) on which Wallace commented.

DISCUSSION

Wallace passed judgement on aspects of religious studies (Hinduism, Christianity), literature (English poetry), classical studies (Greece and Rome), art history (architecture, design), and philosophy (mind). History too is implicated in his denial of mental progress. Only music escapes the sweep of his critical pen.

Such remarks are common. From Wallace's day to this, scientists have routinely explored the humanities. Some have even proposed to annex them. 'What is the domain of Science?' asked a brash young Victorian mathematical physicist. 'It is all possible human knowledge which can rightly be used to guide human conduct' (Clifford, 1879, vol.2, p.70). Which takes in rather a lot. A similar proposal has been made in our own day, to 'turn moral philosophy into an applied science' by using concepts from the new field of sociobiology (which studies the genetic basis of behaviour). Philosophers on the whole are not amused (Ruse and Wilson, 1986).

Scientists are not amused either when outsiders trespass on their domain. They are just as status-conscious, just as jealous of their professional patch as anyone in the humanities. And rightly so. Intruders on science readily confuse or caricature what they don't understand. They need warning, or seeing off. Sometimes, though, scientists overreact to those who merely study what scientists *do*. Such people – sociologists, anthropologists, historians – are accused of ignoring 'the unnatural nature of science' (Wolpert, 1992); they rush in where philosophers fear to tread and draw near to our culture's most potent source of knowledge. This is presumptuous, it is said. Scientific knowledge is not commonsensical but abstruse, even arcane. Science must be revered.

Of course, hard-won knowledge should be respected wherever it is found, and not least when our lives depend on it. What would we do without brain surgery, nutritional analysis, or immunization against disease? Science *is* our provider, our secular providence. But it is not a deity to which we must bow. Science is only a 'golem'.

> A golem is a creature of Jewish mythology. It is a humanoid made by man from clay and water, with incantations and spells. It is powerful. It grows a little more powerful every day. It will follow orders, do your work, and protect you from the ever threatening enemy. But it is clumsy and dangerous. Without control, a golem may destroy its masters with its flailing vigour ... In the mediaeval tradition, the creature of clay was animated by having the Hebrew 'EMETH', meaning truth, inscribed on its forehead – it is truth that drives it on. But this does not mean it understands the truth – far from it.

Golem Science is not an evil creature but it is a little daft. It cannot be blamed for its mistakes because they are our mistakes. It must not be blamed for doing the best it can (Collins and Pinch, 1993, pp.1–2).

Worshipping science, then, is wrong. The Golem is stronger than us but not better. Wariness of science would seem a more appropriate attitude, or perhaps respectful doubt – the kind shown by Her Majesty's loyal opposition when on its best behaviour. Asking parliamentary questions is not treasonous; on the contrary, it may promote better or more open government. Examining science likewise may help us understand the powerful but clumsy creature on which our lives depend.

EXERCISE

Take a historical example. Thomas Carlyle was a Victorian sage and social critic noted for his literary essays and romantic histories – a hard-line humanities man, you might say. Here is part of the opening passage of his famous allegory, *Sartor Resartus*, written about 1830. Some names and allusions may be unfamiliar, but never mind. See if you can simply (1) identify all the sorts of knowledge that Carlyle refers to as being 'kindled' at the 'Torch of Science', and (2) make out his general attitude towards them.

> [T]he Torch of Science ... still burns, and perhaps more fiercely than ever, but innumerable Rush-lights, and Sulphur-matches, kindled thereat, are also glancing in every direction, so that not the smallest cranny or doghole in

Nature or Art can remain unilluminated ... Our Theory of Gravitation is as good as perfect: Lagrange, it is well known, has proved that the Planetary System, on this scheme, will endure forever; Laplace, still more cunningly, even guesses that it could not have been made on any other scheme.

FIGURE 16/17.2
*Thomas Carlyle, 1849.
From J.A. Froude,
Thomas Carlyle, 1882,
London, Longmans,
vol.1, frontispiece*

Whereby, at least, our nautical Logbooks can be better kept; and water-transport of all kinds has grown more commodious. Of Geology and Geognosy we know enough; what with the labours of our Werners and Huttons, what with the ardent genius of their disciples, it has come about that now, to many a Royal Society, the Creation of a World is little more mysterious than the cooking of a Dumpling; concerning which last, indeed, there have been minds to whom the question, *How the Apples were got in* presented difficulties. Why mention our disquisitions on the Social Contract, on the Standard of Taste, on the Migrations of the Herring?

Then, have we not a Doctrine of Rent, a Theory of Value; Philosophies of Language, of History, of Pottery, of Apparitions, of Intoxicating Liquors? Man's whole life and environment have been laid open and elucidated; scarcely a fragment or fibre of his Soul, Body, and Possessions, but has been probed, dissected, distilled, desiccated, and scientifically decomposed: our spiritual Faculties, of which it appears there are not a few, have their Stewarts, Cousins, Royer Collards: every cellular, vascular, muscular Tissue glories in its Lawrences, Magendies, Bichâts.

(Carlyle, 1838, pp.1–2)

DISCUSSION

1   Carlyle refers directly to *astronomy* and *geology*, and indirectly – at the end – to *anatomy* and *physiology*. In between you may have identified *politics* ('Social Contract'), *aesthetics* ('Standard of Taste'), *zoology* ('Migrations of the Herring'), *economics* ('Doctrine of Rent', 'Theory of Value'), *linguistics* ('Philosophies of Language'), *history*, *manufacturing* ('Pottery'), *psychology* ('Apparitions'), and *brewing* ('Intoxicating Liquors').

2   Carlyle's attitude seems flippant. Serious and silly subjects are thrown together without distinction. The art of astronomers, the genius of geologists, and the marvels of medicine are discussed in deep ironic tones. Carlyle was surely no devotee of science.

But what *was* 'science' in 1830? The Latin root *scientia*, meaning knowledge, was familiar to Carlyle. His 'Torch of Science' was the lamp of traditional learning, burning through the ages. It was not *this* 'Science' before which he refused to bow – hardly. He baulked only at all the minor spills and incendiaries, those 'innumerable Rush-lights, and Sulphur-matches' that bid to illuminate even 'the smallest cranny or doghole in Nature or Art'. These together did not amount to Science with a capital 'S'; they were merely derivative little sciences, 'kindled thereat'. Carlyle, like many intellectuals of the time, poked fun at them.

Changing science

Carlyle might be thought to typify the worst of the humanities' attitudes to science. But here again a historical perspective is needed. The world looked very different in 1830. Then there *were* only many sciences, little 'knowledges' claiming to be scientific. (Carlyle's text refers to some of them.) What we now think of as 'Science' – a universal body of expert knowledge based on agreed methods of enquiry – is a cunning abstraction. It obscures the innumerable disputes about knowledge-claims – about what may *count* as science – that took place over centuries. Remember: the Golem at which we marvel was built by human hands. Science today is as much a natural product of history as any religious system.

This is the starting point for work in History of Science: the recognition that science, like religion (and literature, art, philosophy, etc.) is a *historical* subject. Its beliefs, practices, and objects – its very meanings – have changed through time. Always there is human agency. Science has been *made*.

EXERCISE

What then do you think makes History of Science distinctive among the humanities disciplines?

DISCUSSION

You probably answered that the 'science' is distinctive. In History of Science one studies scientific discoveries, scientific institutions, scientific instruments, scientific theories, and scientists themselves. Not poetry, painting, or philosophy.

Or perhaps you recalled the concerns of Wallace and Carlyle. Scientists routinely comment on the humanities; poets, painters, and philosophers often deal with scientific subjects. So you could have answered that the 'science' is what's distinctive about History of Science *wherever it may be found*.

This certainly opens up the discipline, as indeed it has been enlarged for many years. Some of the most stimulating recent work on the history of science has taken poetry and novels, paintings and engravings, and philosophical texts as primary sources. For instance, *Darwin's Plots*

(1983) by Gillian Beer discusses 'evolutionary narrative' in nineteenth-century fiction; *Scenes from Deep Time* (1992) by Martin Rudwick looks into 'early pictorial representations' of prehistory; and *The Invisible World* (1995) by Catherine Wilson studies the connection between 'early modern philosophy and the invention of the microscope'. The sources on which these books draw are richly diverse, but even so the same question must be asked of them all: *whose* science is found there? If science is a historical phenomenon, what may count as 'scientific' in a given source, at a given time?

As we shall see, how one answers this question is crucial to the way the history of science is studied. Indeed, it is precisely this sensitivity to the changing meaning and scope of 'science' that is now most distinctive about the discipline. Unlike other humanities disciplines whose subjects are historical, History of Science specializes in showing how *science* is historical, how it has been *made*.

Let me illustrate. In 1831 the world's first ever scientific roadshow got under way, the British Association for the Advancement of Science. Meeting each year in a different town, it gave specialists a week-long platform before an admiring but largely untutored public. (The show goes on today.) 'Mathematical and physical sciences', 'chemistry', 'mineralogy', 'geology and geography', 'zoology and botany', and 'mechanical arts' were all put on display in polished lectures – by wealthy gents. At the time there were no paid professional careers in science. One had to have means; research was an expensive luxury, or at best a part-time job. The British Association was not set up by a bunch of white-coated boffins. Its founders and leaders were a close-knit group of

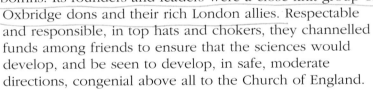

Oxbridge dons and their rich London allies. Respectable and responsible, in top hats and chokers, they channelled funds among friends to ensure that the sciences would develop, and be seen to develop, in safe, moderate directions, congenial above all to the Church of England.

FIGURE 16/17.3 *Reverend William Whewell, 1835. From a lithograph by E.U. Addis. Reproduced by permission of the Royal College of Physicians, London*

Now it was in this genteel circle that a word we take for granted today was first used. In 1833, while gathered at the Anglican stronghold of Cambridge, British Association members were urged to stop calling themselves 'philosophers'. This had been their traditional name – physics was called 'natural philosophy' – but it now seemed lofty and vague. The scientific enterprise as a whole was in danger of losing its intellectual and moral integrity unless Christian astronomers, chemists, geologists, and botanists united under a single banner. A unique 'general term' was needed by which they would all be known. One of the eminent dons present, the polymathic Rev. William Whewell, had the solution. He coined the word 'scientist' to stand for one who studied material nature (Yeo, 1993, pp.110–11).

But Whewell's 'scientist' could not legitimately study all that scientists do today. For instance, there could be no full-scale cosmogony, no 'Big Bang' theory or 'brief history of time'; no science of life's origin and evolution; no psychology or models of the mind. These subjects were taboo and out-of-bounds. The origin of the universe, the evolution of life, and the operation of the mind were all said to depend on *spiritual* causes that lay outside the scope of the sciences. Such causes were the province of theology and its specialists, the clergy. God created the universe and life; the soul believed and prayed. Neither God nor the soul could be calculated, experimented on, or subjected to 'natural law'. To pretend otherwise was not merely unorthodox; it could mean professional ruin.

Cracks appeared in the British Association's formidable front but none was catastrophic. What kept the gents together, as much as anything, was

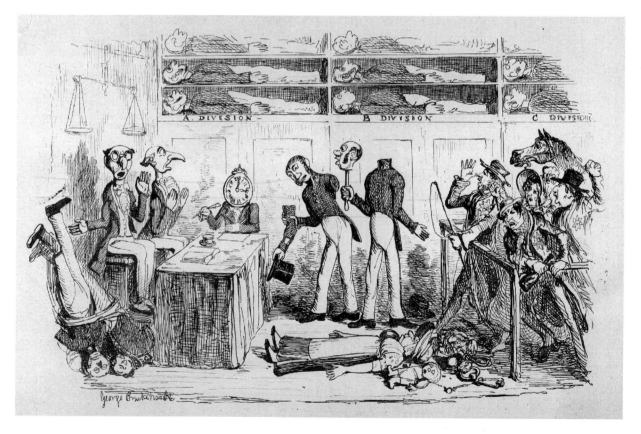

FIGURE 16/17.4 'The Automaton Police Office': a satirical drawing by George Cruikshank first printed in Bentley's *Miscellany*, vol.4, 1838, p.209. Cruikshank mocks the scientists displaying their mechanical wares (here automaton constables in 'divisions' A through C, that is, the British Association 'sections' devoted to physics, chemistry, and geology), as well as the police authority itself (note the jeering crowd). The cartoon accompanied a report by Charles Dickens sending up a 'Meeting of the Mudfog Association for the Advancement of Everything'. Reproduced by permission of the British Library Board their aversion for the crackpots outside. These men and women called themselves 'radicals' and many were politically motivated. To them the British Association was the British Ass. Fringe GPs, itinerant lecturers, religious zealots, low-brow publishers, self-taught hawkers and hacks – their social status was as dubious as their scientific pretensions. (Wallace was typical, as you'll see.) They spread dangerous knowledge and sponsored do-it-yourself research. They tended to favour democracy. They taught the wrong things to the wrong people in the wrong places at the wrong times.

Take the 'nebular hypothesis', for instance, the grand speculation that the planets of our solar system condensed as molten droplets from a whirling fiery mist. Or 'phrenology', the homely belief that cranial bumps are the key to brain structure and thus to human character. Or 'mesmerism' (now hypnotism), the supposition that one mind may control another through the medium of an invisible force or fluid. Or 'transmutation' (now evolution), the foul French notion that plants and animals, including 'man', developed progressively from dirt. To the British Association élite

FIGURE 16/17.5   *A sketch of the spiral nebula found in 1845 using the Earl of Rosse's gigantic 6-foot reflecting telescope at Parsonstown in Ireland. When this powerful, state-of-the-art instrument failed to 'resolve' the whirlpool of light into discrete stars, supporters of the nebular hypothesis used it as evidence of the 'progressive' changes through which the Solar System had evolved. From J.P. Nichol,* Thoughts on Some Important Points relating to the System of the World, *2nd edn, 1848, Edinburgh, J. Johnstone, p.73. Reproduced by permission of the British Library Board*

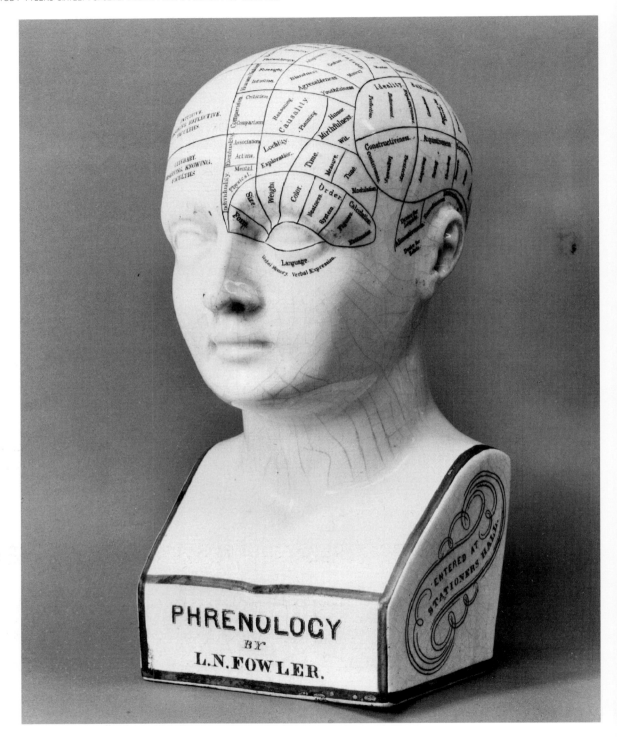

FIGURE 16/17.6 *Phrenology bust, showing the location of the brain's underlying 'organs'. 'Getting your head examined' was the nineteenth-century equivalent of today's genetic fingerprinting. Lorenzo Niles Fowler and his family, all Americans, probably did more to popularize phrenology in Britain after 1860 than any other practitioners. Reproduced by permission of the Wellcome Institute Library, London*

all such doctrines oozed from the same quagmire on the lunatic fringe. They were plebian heresies and undermined spiritual authority. They were 'unscience', 'pseudo-science', or 'anti-science'. (Carlyle of course agreed.)

Science has moved on. Nebular development is now accepted, brain functions have been localized, hypnotism is available on the NHS, and evolution knows no bounds. Old heresies have been accommodated, spiritual things cast out. The sciences of the early British Association have been revamped and enlarged beyond its members' wildest dreams or fears. Science today – with a capital 'S' – accounts for everything by causes within the *material* world.

Explaining change

Why the enormous change in British science from the 1830s to the 1990s? Historians have been puzzling out the story for years. Their conclusions vary, but on one point most now agree. The change did not take place automatically. Nor was it driven by mere force of facts. Even that great engine, the Victorian economy, was a paltry power, too slow and awkward to set every research horizon. What changed science was the combined actions of individuals and groups – armed with 'facts', of course, and responsive to economic needs – competing with one another, striving for goals such as 'truth', 'freedom', 'democracy', 'efficiency', and 'the common good'. The outcome – Science today – was no more inevitable than, say, the rise of universal suffrage or the collapse of Soviet communism. Rewind the tape of history, delete a crucial vote, miss out a few discoveries, let a 'great man' die young, give or take a war, then replay: Science would look different – possibly as different as early Victorian science looks to us.

EXERCISE

Think back to Block 3 and your study of the French Revolution. There you also learned about social and political pressures, and how events might have turned out otherwise. Is it really the same with our knowledge of the natural world? Can you think of one factor that might make the development of science *entirely different* from, say, the overthrow of Louis XVI or the coming of the Terror?

DISCUSSION

You could say that what differentiates scientific change from political change is the part played by the *natural world*. After all, the natural world doesn't behave like the French Assembly or Robespierre. It changes in regular ways and so can be predicted and controlled.

This point is crucial. Many scholars, especially scientists, believe that it sets the history of science apart from other kinds of history. 'In political changes', says an eminent American zoologist, 'succeeding governments often have diametrically opposed objectives and ideologies, while in a succession of theories dealing with the same scientific problem each step benefits from the new insights acquired by the preceding step and builds on it' (Mayr, 1990, p.302). Scientific knowledge, then, is cumulative and progressive, politics chaotic. Why? Because 'science always relates to the outside world,' writes a well-known British biologist; 'its success depends on how well its theories correspond with reality'. Under other historical conditions 'the *course* of science would have been very different, but the *ideas* would have ended up the same' because there is only one 'reality' for them to correspond to. 'Science, despite blips and errors, more and more provides an understanding of the world' (Wolpert, 1992, pp.2, 121; emphasis added).

These are impressive arguments, but historians of science today feel bound to analyse rather than just accept them. Obviously the arguments show what 'science' means to scientists – cumulative, progressive, and 'real' knowledge of nature – and this view predominates in Western cultures. Just as obviously the arguments fail to represent what other people, including experts, thought about science in other times and places.

Again, let me illustrate from history. In the later Middle Ages astronomical theory was actually *divorced* from 'reality'. The Earth was believed to be at the centre of the universe but the skies were a geometer's junkyard, littered with hypothetical machinery – 'equants', 'deferents', 'epicycles' – by which astronomers calculated the positions of the planets. The *real* existence of these devices was irrelevant to predicting, say, where Venus would turn up next, and successful predictions were made. After Copernicus sent the Earth spinning round the Sun, however, the *same* predictions were made on the basis of vastly *different* ideas about the universe. Copernicus believed that his astronomy was physically real, not just a calculating device, and in time most educated people agreed. Theory and reality began to converge (as we now believe), but not because the new science was more successful at making predictions.

In nineteenth-century astronomy the reality of other things was in dispute. Were there in fact great gaseous nebulae whirling in the heavens, or could more powerful telescopes resolve the cosmic clouds into innumerable distant stars? Could some such cloud have condensed to form our solar system? What indeed did it mean for the nebular theory of origins to 'correspond' to reality when the only evidence for that supposed reality – aeons of development – lay in present-day observations? Was it even a 'theory', or merely a 'hypothesis', as Whewell called it? Who should decide?

Similar questions were posed about nineteenth-century psychology and evolutionary biology. My point is not that cogent answers were lacking but simply that informed people disagreed. Like politicians, scientists *did* have 'diametrically opposed objectives and ideologies'; it was by no means certain at any time whose 'science' would prevail, the British Association's, say, or the radicals'. If, however, external reality had *imposed* the answers, if 'facts' had coerced, there would have been no controversy. All informed people (including awkward Mr Wallace) would have agreed about what should count as science. All informed people would agree today – *if* the natural world determined the ways in which we understand it. But informed people differ profoundly about what the world is like (never mind other folks); scientists do so notoriously. In the 1990s experts testifying about the DNA evidence in the O.J. Simpson criminal trial contradicted one another before a world-wide television audience; European medics and veterinarians argued about the risks of contracting the human equivalent of BSE ('mad cow disease') by eating British beef. Indeed, the ruckus in the late 1980s over 'cold fusion' (generating nuclear power in a test-tube) showed that scientists may even disagree about *how* their disagreements should be aired – where, by whom, and when.

Now all these problems are broadly 'political' – problems of achieving consent. They make the history of science more like other kinds of history than a record of cumulative progress. This is not to say that there can't be a consensus among those who study nature, or that 'facts' are unimportant in forming the consensus. When we speak abstractly of 'Science' we testify indirectly to the remarkable agreement that *does* exist among researchers. What I and other historians maintain is only that this agreement is the product of controversy, negotiation, and persuasion – pressures like those at work in ordinary politics.

The usual way out of politics for those who think the history of science is unique is to start boldly from the present: take 'science' to be what we *now* know is true and study the past in its light. Every theory, every researcher, every institution then turns out to be on either the 'right track' or the 'wrong track', either steaming towards present-day truth or straying onto sidings. Only *real* science progresses because that's what we *mean* by science. In this view, medieval astronomy would be science side-tracked, an intellectual dead-end. The nebular hypothesis would be a great leap forward, though scientists shunned it in the early British Association. Belief in divine creation, which was universal among the same scientists, would however be seen as anti-science. The litmus test: science today.

EXERCISE

If you were to *explain* scientific change on the two-track model: (1) What would be the engine of progress in our knowledge of nature? (2) What would interfere with such progress, causing diversions or derailments?

DISCUSSION

1   You might explain scientific progress by the accumulation of hard evidence, or *facts*. Facts are used to prove or disprove things, so *reason* would have to come in, pursuing *truth*. What's proven true – scientific *ideas* – also needs accounting for. You might well follow some scientists and ascribe these ideas to that 'almost total mystery', scientific *genius* (Wolpert, 1992, p.67). Facts fuel the juggernaut of science but genius is at the throttle.

2   Scientific progress might be slowed by the sheer difficulty of certain problems (say, the structure of the atom), but what interferes with progress – holds it up, stands in the way – would be human failings: *superstition, lies, prejudice, stupidity*, and the like. You might have answered simply 'religion' and said it all. For over a century the 'conflict of religion and science' has been seen as the chief hindrance to scientific progress in the Western world. Religion is said to have institutionalized 'irrationality', making intellectual 'crimes' into social and political ones. The persecution of Galileo in the seventeenth century and of Darwin in the nineteenth – the brute tenacity of their assailants – is routinely ascribed to this 'extra-scientific' factor.

With many variations and refinements the history of science in the West was largely written on the two-track model from the 1930s to the 1970s. The model's heyday came during the Cold War, when Soviet communism threatened the autonomy of science and the integrity of the arts. Historians of science, keen to keep their own house in order, began labelling one another 'externalists' and 'internalists'.

An *externalist* was typically (but not necessarily) a Marxist who abandoned the two-track model and sought to explain scientific progress by 'external' or extra-scientific factors such as class interest and economic need. A Marxist historian accepted that at one level progress results from rational enquiry – observation, experiment, and so on – which religion always thwarts. But rational enquiry itself was seen as part of a progressive historical struggle leading to a classless society. Marxism gave the 'scientific' explanation of this movement, and of course some Marxists – henchmen of Joseph Stalin – sought to further it through the political control of research.

'Bunk!' cried internalists. Marxism is not scientific; its beliefs about historical change are themselves quasi-religious. Such irrational beliefs can never explain what is rational. Nature yields nothing to political pressure. Only error results – pseudo-science or ideology. The Soviet Union furnished choice examples.

An *internalist* upheld the two-track model, defending an autonomous or 'internal' logic of science. In this view, truth is discovered by following rational rules of engagement with nature: making hypotheses, drawing out consequences, testing them – the 'scientific method' you learned about in school. When a scientist 'does what is rational to do, we need enquire no further into the causes of his action; whereas, when he does what is in fact irrational – even if he believes it to be rational – we require some further explanation' (Laudan, 1977, p.189). Only then may 'external' factors like religion or politics be invoked in the history of science: to explain why falsehoods are accepted – why researchers go 'off the rails'.

History of Science has moved on at the end of the twentieth century. The discipline has undergone a change comparable to that of the sciences themselves since the early days of the British Association. Externalist–internalist talk is dying; science is now seen as an integral part of culture. No doubt this change too was conditioned by political events, from the upheavals of the 1960s to the end of the Cold War. But that is a matter for future historians. What we must do now, before returning to Wallace, is to look closer at two key principles that inform the study of the history of science today.

Naturalism and symmetry

Let's go back to our starting point: the recognition that science is historical and as much a *natural* human creation – a golem – as any religious system (p.90). If you hadn't noticed, that last clause is controversial. Many religious people would disagree passionately. To them what it means to be religious is to believe just the opposite: that their ideas about the world are ultimately *supernatural* in origin, revealed by God and permanently true. Any suggestion that these are mere human creations – golems, idols – would be *ir*religious.

You may of course have your own view, but whatever it is, the supernaturalist conviction must be taken seriously. I say so not just because it is one by which millions today live and die, but also because it has an exact parallel in the way most people regard scientific knowledge. Examining this parallel will clarify the two principles, *naturalism* and *symmetry*, observed by historians of science. Later you will be asked to apply the principles to key episodes in Wallace's career.

Natural explanations of religious ideas are typically offered by 'outsiders' rather than 'insiders', which is one reason they provoke controversy. Believers insist that to understand a religion properly one must be 'within the fold', committed, trusting in supernatural agencies and events. But as you learned in the last two units, there is much to be gained from an outsider perspective. Religious Studies takes a 'critical' and 'impartial' approach, ignoring the limitations imposed by 'theology', and the first theology set aside as the discipline expanded was that of the Christian churches (pp.44–6).

FIGURE 16/17.7   *Ferdinand Christian Baur, the Protestant professor of New Testament, church history, and history of dogma at Tübingen University from 1826 until his death in 1860. From a painting by Emil Kornbeck, by courtesy of the Mansell Collection/Time Inc., New York*

Christians had long believed the Bible to be a revelation of divine truth, but in the early nineteenth century German academics began studying it critically and impartially, just like secular writings had been. Ferdinand Baur of Tübingen University led a group of scholars who, using the most advanced data and techniques available, rewrote the early history of Christianity. The 'Tübingen School' treated the development of theology like any other historical movement. Those who believed that biblical truths had emerged under the guidance of supernatural power were seen to be partial and one-sided.

> As Baur explained ... 'supernaturalists' divide the history of dogma into two parts which are treated in different ways. One part is the record of authentically apostolic truth. This flows from divine sources, and needs no other explanation beyond its divinity. The other part is the record of heresy and doctrinal deviation. This is to be accounted for by everything that can cloud the vision of the faithful and lead them astray. Here explanation is in terms of ambition, greed, ignorance, superstition and evil. We are fallen creatures, and this explains deviations from the path of true dogmatic development.
>
> *(Bloor, 1992, p.184)*

EXERCISE

Supernaturalists explained religious truth and error in *different* ways. Truth to them was God's *supernatural* gift, error the product of *natural* human failings. What does this two-fold approach to Christian history remind you of?

DISCUSSION

I hope you thought immediately of the two-track model as held by internalist historians of science. According to this model, the discovery of truth is sufficiently explained by scientists' rational grasp of reality; when error prevails it is to be ascribed to external, irrational or non-scientific factors.

The Tübingen alternative to supernaturalist history was not entirely new, but the rigour with which Baur pursued it was certainly original, as were the results.

> Baur exhibited what would now be called the 'social construction' of the New Testament. He showed how its doctrinal content emerged from the competing interests of different Church parties, and described their strategies of negotiation and compromise. In his study of the varying relations between the Pauline and Petrine parties in the early Church [those associated with the apostles Paul and Peter], Baur showed the importance of locating what he called the 'tendency' of a text, that is, the purpose and interest that informed it ... [He] did not seek to decide whether the tendencies he described were theologically correct. Nor did he pass judgement on the inner authenticity of the religious life of historical actors ... For Baur, Church history only made sense when fully integrated into the realm of historical causes and effects. Christian doctrine was an historical product, transmitted from generation to generation and interpreted afresh in the light of new circumstances. The Divine forces informing that doctrine were not qualitatively different from the power behind all human and natural processes ...
>
> *(Bloor, 1988, pp.59–60)*

EXERCISE

Baur and the Tübingen School treated the history of Christian dogma as a purely *natural* development. All doctrines, whether true or false, were to be explained in the *same* way, as the products of ordinary 'historical causes and effects'.

Now see if you can apply this approach to the history of *scientific* knowledge. How would it differ from (1) the internalist and (2) the externalist–Marxist ones? (Try not to read on until you've thought out an answer).

DISCUSSION

1   The Tübingen approach would be even-handed, unlike internalist history of science. Explanations of scientific truth and error would take the same form – they would be *symmetrical*. All knowledge of nature would be shown to emerge from 'competing' interest groups through 'negotiation and compromise', regardless of its correctness.

2   The Tübingen approach, unlike externalist–Marxist history, would not posit an underlying social and political movement – the class struggle – of which the progress of science was a necessary outcome. This would smack of supernaturalism. (Here internalist critics were shrewd: the Marxist 'science' of history does look rather like traditional Christian teaching, with the class struggle driving society forward, replacing divine providence.)

To sum up: Baur and the Tübingen School stood for *naturalism* in history, which required that explanations of truth and error have *symmetry*. Since no non-natural agency guaranteed that certain beliefs were true, ordinary causes and effects had to explain them; and the same kind of explanations applied whether a belief was held to be true or false. This approach to early church history may or may not strike you as fair, but for his part Baur remained a devout believer, deeply convinced that the Christian tradition witnessed to divine truth. He even hoped, ironically, that his impartial research would strengthen and enlarge that tradition and defend it from philosophical attacks. He was a member of God's 'loyal opposition'.

Even so, traditional supernaturalists accused Baur of destroying Christianity. He made it common, like any other movement, they said; he ignored the power of Christ and his word. How could the early church have resolved its differences by mere negotiation and compromise? Is that how the great Christian creeds came into existence? 'Why ... are theological controversies and party conflicts ever resolved if there is not a Divine Reality that eventually impresses itself on the minds of those concerned?' (Bloor, 1988, p.70). This Reality, not finite human judgement, was for supernaturalists the ultimate source of truth.

Such objections were overruled. Naturalism and symmetry became premises of modern historical scholarship.

Today historians of science (like academics in religious studies) try to examine their culture's most cherished beliefs critically and impartially, in the same way that Baur and his colleagues examined theirs. They question 'the unnatural nature of science' (Wolpert, 1992) and seek to account *naturally* for the 'mystery' of scientific genius. They believe in the reality of the external world no less than Baur believed in the reality of God, but just as Baur refused to use God to explain the development of divine truth, so they deny that nature somehow mysteriously determines the ways in which scientists understand it. What comes to be seen as 'true' in science must be explained in the same way as, or *symmetrically* with, what comes to be seen as 'false'. What counts as true is the outcome of natural human processes; 'the truth is not the cause of that outcome' (Collins, 1992, p.186).

Scientists sometimes accuse historians who take this view of being 'anti-science', just as Baur himself was slated for being anti-Christian. But historians reply with Baur that to omit human agency at any point would indeed make their subject unnatural and therefore unhistorical. Many also see themselves as part of a loyal opposition, always questioning where science comes from, always asking 'How?' 'What for?' and 'Why?' A golem that has been made may be improved.

Beyond boundaries: contexts

We've come full circle, back to 'no trespassing' and the humanities' engagement with science (pp.87–90). Science should now look more open to you, historically speaking, than it did at the start. Not only has its meaning changed; so also have its boundaries. The early Victorians drew the lines in one way, scientists today draw them in another. Internalist historians observed the latter lines, arguing that the 'science' one could be external or internal *to* at any time was properly defined in the present. But the internalists' two-track histories lacked naturalism and symmetry; they succumbed to further scholarship. With their passing, the boundary question has been reopened, and you may now well ask: are the insides and the outsides of science completely fluid? Is science all at sea?

Obviously not. You cannot get a Ph.D. from the Open University for a thesis about the power of prayer on plants. You cannot obtain a Royal Society research grant to conduct experiments proving the Earth is flat. You cannot practise voodoo in an NHS hospital. Boundaries remain. But what makes History of Science awkward, especially for scientists, is that it does not take the boundaries for granted (much less does it presume to draw its own). Instead, historians today see the boundaries of science as constructs or conventions. They interrogate primary sources to find out where and how the lines have been drawn.

You can see now why the symmetry principle is so important. Two-track history, which explained truth in one way and error in another, had to know *in advance* what should count as science. It assumed today's boundaries and judged the past accordingly. But this was unfair to historical 'actors'. It made them heroes or villains of progress instead of players in local rep. The actors themselves – people like Mr Wallace – drew different boundaries, over which dramatic confrontations took place. One's truth-claim was another's falsehood across a shifting line.

Nor can history pick and choose among the claimants without privileging someone's boundary. This would place others beyond the pale, making their voices less audible. Knowledge-claims on *all* sides must be explained symmetrically, without respect to who was *or is now* thought to be 'orthodox' or 'heretical', right or wrong. It is the processes by which actors come to agree, and the ways their agreements become conventional, that interest historians. Remember: History of Science specializes in showing *how* science is historical, how it has been *made*. This includes its boundaries.

EXERCISE

'Hang on a second!' (I hear a loud voice.) *'A lot of ghastly things have been done in the name of science. Do you mean to tell us that History of Science has no standpoint or frame of reference for judging them? Is one*

permitted to say nothing as a historian *about the thousands of excruciating experiments performed on live animals in the eighteenth century, or the tens of thousands of useless surgeries performed on women in the nineteenth, or the millions of hapless victims in the twentieth century's mad pursuit of racial purity, nuclear supremacy, and mind control? If we may not use our own intellectual and moral standards in writing about past science, whose are we to use? Or are we, in the name of symmetry, merely to shrug and deal coolly with 'all sides'?*

How would you respond? (There is no 'correct' answer but you might like to consult pp.87–90.)

DISCUSSION

Of course, History of Science has no single view on matters of truth and morality, any more than other arts disciplines do. Individuals may have their own views, but not whole disciplines. Now everyone who studies the past is influenced by the present; historians, being experts on past cultural influences, are particularly well placed to identify present ones (as you learned in Unit 8). Above all, they should be able to recognize how their own beliefs and attitudes – their cultural 'standpoints' – influence their written history. The only question is how *far* one's standpoint necessarily affects reconstructions of the past. Some historians (like the author of Unit 8) compare themselves to natural scientists and defend the autonomy and the objectivity of their writing. Others fault them for failing to take up committed standpoints.

The historical approach to science I've sketched can hardly claim to be 'scientific' (even in the restricted sense of Unit 8) without begging the question of what should count as 'science'. Yet, ironically, this approach too has been criticized for 'morally neutering history', for making it appear 'irrelevant to contemporary moral issues and crises' (King, 1995, p.232). My interlocutor above, shouting 'Hang on a second!', drives the point home.

I wonder. Can't symmetric analyses have asymmetric results? Explaining how magicians perform tricks doesn't impugn their skill, but only deprives it of mystery. Explaining what scientists do doesn't impugn their expertise, but only keeps us from asking more of it than can be expected. And if evil science is what they do, we learn how what not to do is done, which may prevent its repetition. Golem Science works best when watched.

The resources for writing history of science today are not seen as *either* 'internal' *or* 'external' to science. They are not *either* scientific discoveries, theories, and instruments on the one hand, *or* social practices, political ideas, and religious beliefs on the other. How could they be when what's 'internal' or 'external' is always the question in history – what may count as 'science'? The resources historians now use are instead called *contextual*. They are as rich and varied as the historical *contexts* in which knowledge of nature has been made. Nothing of human interest is ruled out. Galileo's court culture, Kepler's music, Newton's numismatics, Darwin's novel-reading, Faraday's fundamentalism, Einstein's civil service career – all are part of *contextualist* history of science. So too equally are the 'scientific' things that scientists do: weighing and measuring, counting and calculating, collecting and exploring, looking up telescopes and down microscopes, writing papers, giving lectures, and applying for grants. Institutions are also vital – observatories and laboratories, colleges and clubs – and of course scientific instruments, the tools of the trade, from astrolabes to atom-smashers.

You don't have to be a scientist to study the history of science but you do need a historical outlook, an ability to understand the past as far as possible on its own terms rather than those of the present (see Block 3, p.54). Our changing knowledge of nature is a cultural process, not merely a cerebral one. Understanding it brings into play all the humanities skills you possess. Poets and painters, philosophers and scientists – each interprets nature in their own tongue with signs, symbols, and speech. The language of science is different but not unique. It too offers a shifting kaleidoscope through which, from age to age, nature appears fearfully and wonderfully made. Scientists do not *present* a perfect mirror-image of nature any more than artists do; instead they *re-present* it in creative and compelling ways, using formulas and texts, drawings and maps. These 'representations' are the art of science and their history is open to all.

3 HERO AND ANTI-HERO

The artistry of science is made most memorable through biography. Who can forget the charming tales in the Ladybird 'Lives of the Great Scientists'? Or the sumptuous TV biopics about Oppenheimer and the Bomb, Rosalind Franklin and DNA, the voyage of Charles Darwin, and the tortured Sigmund Freud? All these portraits, great and small, strengthen one of our culture's commonest perceptions: that of the scientist as hero. Complex he or she may be: wracked by conscience, driven by ambition, tragically slighted or overlooked. Nevertheless, like a lone mountaineer, the scientist-hero inspires and lifts our thoughts, leading us to new vistas of progress. This notion is deeply imbedded in the folk consciousness of modernity. Seventy years on, Amelia Defries's *Pioneers of Science* still says it all, with its jaunty 'pictures of struggle and victory' among 'the living, by whose wisdom we progress', and among 'the dead, by whose light we live' (1928, p.[v]).

Heroes need human challenges as well as natural ones, men to master as well as mountains. Such is the drama of discovery, endlessly scripted in our time. The scientist must have an adversary – an evil institution like 'the church' or a corrupt individual, preferably a politician. This then becomes his stumbling-block, frustrating free enquiry, impeding progress. Or a rival scientist may equally fit the bill: a vainglorious upstart, a grandiloquent imposter, a muddle-headed friend. Heroism consists in surmounting all such obstacles and, shunning self-pride and pretence, pursuing nature wherever 'she' may lead.

High in the first division of scientific heroes is the 'Newton of natural history', Charles Darwin (1809–82). It was he who slowly and methodically, with infinite patience and perseverance, single-handedly solved that 'mystery of mysteries', how living species originate. Or so hero-worshippers say. And, of course, to them Darwin had fiendish foes – bishops mostly, the odd politician, countless minor bigots – who fought

FIGURE 16/17.8 *'A Sun of the Nineteenth Century': Charles Darwin banishing bishops, Bibles, and priestly hobgoblins. From Puck (New York), 3 May 1882, in Darwin Archive 215.35, Cambridge University Library. Reproduced by permission of the Syndics of Cambridge University Library*

in vain to stem the tide of truth. Less is heard about Darwin's professional rivals. Science with a capital 'S' is supposed to be united; in heroic history only renegades break ranks. Yet noted Victorian scientists did break ranks, publicly and conspicuously, and one of them is routinely cast as Darwin's opposite number, our friend Alfred Russel Wallace (1823–1913).

Not that he is all ogre. As often as Wallace is made a whipping-boy or laughing-stock he is the genial seer or saint. Winsome and likeable, he sometimes plays constructive parts – the resourceful Tonto to Darwin's Lone Ranger, or the helpful Watson to Sherlock Holmes. Even so, Wallace remains the anti-hero. In all roles he is a foil, a lesser light reflecting a greater glory. One biographer actually dubs him 'Darwin's moon' (Williams-Ellis, 1966).

Was he a lunatic then? Hardly. Wallace is made a mere satellite because of his part in one of the most poignant ironies in the history of science. In February 1858 he had the brilliant misfortune to hit on the central premise of modern biology, the theory on which the whole field now rests – evolution by 'natural selection' – *twenty years too late.* Unknown to him, Darwin, working privately, had got there first, and when he heard of Wallace's ideas a few months later he scooped the kudos by rushing into print with his famous book *On the Origin of Species* (1859). Wallace, his originality eclipsed, remained the perfect gent but stubbornly went his own way. Within a decade he and Darwin had parted company on a range of issues. Most remarkably, Wallace came out as a spiritualist and socialist. On both counts he played the crank to Darwin's correctness (it was said) and 'lost caste terribly' (Colp, 1992, p.11). Only as an afterthought was he asked in 1882 to bear Darwin's coffin in Westminster Abbey.

EXERCISE

Wallace is still remembered (if at all) as an afterthought and also-ran. He is a casualty of our preoccupation with scientific heroes. But in historical writing about Wallace other assumptions are apparent, and you should now be able to spot them. Please answer the following questions from the extracts below:

1   In a word, what explanation does each passage suggest for Wallace's diminished reputation? unorthodox. Misguided.

2   Which passages best exemplify: (a) internalist or 'two-track' history? A + D. (b) contextualist history? C.

3   What attitude to the Wallace–Darwin relationship do *all* the passages share? Acknowledge his achievements Sympathetic.

[A] Although this [spiritualist] nonsense of Wallace's caused a rift in his tenuous association with Darwin, hindering perhaps the forward march of evolution, the two men remained friends. Despite the fact that as he grew older, Wallace became even more misguided and for a time was almost ostracised for his unorthodox beliefs, he and Darwin remained in contact; Darwin, who had always been grateful for Wallace's magnanimity over the priority of discovery issue, managed somehow to tolerate Wallace's aberration.

(*White and Gribbin, 1995, p.233*)

[B] Darwin I believe is the greatest naturalist who has ever lived … I am anxious, in this brief history of thought leading up to our present views, to give Wallace what I feel to be a rather fairer proportion of the credit for the history of [natural] selection than has usually been allotted him outside strictly biological circles … For all the patient labour in preparing the case and for its masterly presentation Darwin must get the greater credit, but for brilliance of insight Wallace, I believe, should get more acknowledgement than he has received.

(*Hardy, 1984, pp.60–61, 64*)

[C] A man's following is not so much the sum of all the people who favour his various ideas as it is the residue left after subtracting all those whom he has affronted by one or another. Subtract the gentlemen and those of vested financial interests who were shocked by Wallace's socialism, the scientists who scoffed at spiritualism … and the conservative religious folk who were shocked by evolution – and who is left to sing Wallace's praises? It is small wonder we have almost forgotten his part in belling the cat.

(*Hardin, 1960, p.45*)

[D] Perhaps Darwin oversimplified the problem. He certainly approached it in the proper manner, and there is no doubt that he understood the logical issues. Darwin and Wallace exchanged a series of letters in which the whole question is clearly formulated. Wallace went to extreme lengths … but Darwin was unconvinced by these efforts, and rightly so, for they were exceedingly farfetched. The dispute is particularly revealing, for it casts much light on their respective attitudes toward methodology and metaphysics … The same kind of disagreement, with Wallace and with others, occurs in various contexts, clearly demonstrating Darwin's superiority as a theoretician over his contemporaries. It was because of Darwin's innate capacity for logic that he had to remark to Wallace: 'We shall, I greatly fear, never agree'.

(*Ghiselin, 1969, pp.150–51*)

DISCUSSION

1   Wallace's reputation has suffered (A) because he was 'misguided', believing in spiritualism; (B) because his work has been underrated 'outside strictly biological circles' and, by implication, because he was less patient than Darwin and his presentation fell short; (C) because he offended so many people; and (D) because his science was inferior to Darwin's, being poorly conceived and argued.

2   I hope you identified passages A and D as examples of internalist or two-track history. In passage A, beliefs about spiritualism are treated *a*symmetrically, as if they had a different explanation to that of true science. Darwin's scientific scepticism is assumed to be correct; he is said to have tolerated Wallace's 'aberration', though this 'nonsense' may have caused a rift that hindered 'the forward march of evolution'. The boundaries between science and non-science, the rational and the irrational, are simply assumed to be fixed where scientists today – following Darwin himself – place them.

Passage D alludes to Wallace's spiritualism ('metaphysics') but is mainly concerned to point up his logical lapses in science. He went to 'extreme lengths' over an unspecified 'problem' (the origin of sexual sterility); his replies to Darwin were 'exceedingly farfetched'. Their 'dispute', however, reveals nothing about how scientific controversies are conducted, but only Darwin's 'innate capacity for logic', which Wallace himself lacked. Such appeal to genius is typical of the old internalist history.

Passage B is ambiguous. Its reference to history 'leading up to our present views' does suggest the two-track approach (a point strengthened by the dedication of the book in which it appears, 'with homage to the genius of Alfred Russel Wallace'!) but there is also the hint that Wallace's work may have suffered 'outside' biology for lack of fair exposure. This suggests a less internal, more socially nuanced account of Wallace's status.

Only passage C evokes a contextualist interpretation. Here everyone occupies a level pitch where players' opinions cancel one another. Wallace's reputation is seen as the product of the competition. The next step would be to apply the same analysis to Wallace's science, although the author, a scientist working in the 1950s, was unable to follow through.

3   All the passages have a strong moralizing tone. They assess who was better or worse, superior or inferior, right or wrong. The question is always how much 'praise' Wallace or Darwin deserves, how much 'credit' the one should get relative to the other. This perfectly illustrates the perils of judging past science by today's standards or backing one side in a historical boundary dispute. The sense of

science's *making*, of how boundaries came to *exist*, and of *how* Wallace and Darwin ended up on opposite sides, is lost by assuming in advance what 'science' should mean.

Internalist history is implicitly heroic, its players 'right' or 'wrong'. It takes sides. Contextualist history is anti-heroic, not because it favours anti-heroes, but simply because it gives them a voice. It levels the pitch and lets everyone join in. The contextualist writer is not a referee, imposing today's rules on the past. One is rather like a commentator, following the game of science as it was played, explaining strategies, describing the drama, the brilliant saves, the own goals. The rules sometimes change, the goalposts move. Uproar ensues. Rival fans invade the pitch. Players are sent off and substitutions made. Order is somehow restored. The game goes on and its present state-of-play is known. But in contextualist history this knowledge does not skew the commentary. The match could have gone differently. By now another side might have been winning. Or in future perhaps another *will* be – who knows?

Only contextualist history can deal fairly with all aspects of Wallace's long and colourful career. In the remaining pages I want you study it in this way – to *practise* what historians of science today preach. Proceeding biographically, we start by exploring the wider context of Wallace's most famous moment, his discovery of natural selection in 1858. Then we'll examine his latter-day spiritualism and socialism.

4 WALLACE THE SURVEYOR

After failing in business Wallace's father moved his impoverished family from London to Usk in Monmouthshire (now Gwent), where in 1823 the eighth child, Alfred Russel, was born. Their cottage stood on the west side of the River Usk, the town itself on the east. Alfred never forgot the scenic walk into town, over the old three-arched bridge a quarter-mile away. Crossing it, he would stop and peer upstream to catch a glimpse of 'the mountains near Abergavenny, ten miles off'. These, he had heard, marked 'the beginning of the unknown land of Wales'. The locals spoke Welsh and in town they called him 'the "little Saxon"' for his long blonde hair (Wallace, 1905, vol.1, pp.24, 29). Ethnic differences and natural boundaries were impressed on him from early childhood.

At the age of five Alfred moved with his family back to England. He attended Hertford Grammar School, then in 1837 went to live with his brother John, a builder's apprentice in London. The teenage boys spent evenings at the workingmen's 'Hall of Science' just off Tottenham Court Road. The coffee was free and the lectures stirring, with tirades against private property and religion. Here Alfred picked up the political values that stayed with him more or less for life: human nature is perfectible through education and changed environments; all humans are equal partners in progress. So taught the industrial reformer Robert Owen, whom Alfred once heard lecture. He left town that summer, a budding socialist, to join his big brother William in Bedfordshire as a trainee land surveyor.

It was a boom time for the trade. The year before, Parliament had ended the age-old right of farmers to pay tithes in kind. A 'rent charge' was substituted, based on the average value of titheable produce and the productive quality of the land. The charge was apportioned property-by-property or field-by-field, and required an accurate survey. Squads of transit-toting, chain-lugging young men were hired. Their maps had legal status and the format was prescribed. Exact boundaries had to be shown, quantities calculated, and the quality or use of land assessed. Tithe owners pored over every detail, anxious to secure their due. Tenant farmers fumed. The rent charge was a tax on gross output, just like the old tithe. The harder they worked, the fatter the squire or the parson.

Young Wallace paced the open fields, revelling in the fresh air and trigonometry. He knew the 'well-to-do farmers' but mostly mixed with 'labourers' and 'mechanics' in pubs. Here poaching songs were sung and grievances aired. His political education went on. In 1839 the brothers moved to the Welsh borders to make parish maps and survey for the enclosure of commons. This dividing up of open land among landowners was also bitterly resented. Peasants lost their ancient grazing rights and had to pay for them instead. 'Legalized robbery of the poor for the aggrandisement of the rich', Wallace later called it, though at the time he simply assumed that, however unpopular, it had '*some* right and reason' (1905, vol.1, pp.124, 151, 158).

From 'Becca to Malthus

In 1841 the brothers pushed on into the 'unknown land of Wales'. Wallace now first immersed himself in the culture, lodging in pubs, attending chapels, and admiring 'the grand sound of the language'. The surveying continued, and late that autumn they arrived at Neath in Glamorganshire to map an enormous parish. They lived and boarded for a year with a 'rather rough' hill farmer, himself the bailiff of the 4,000-acre Duffryn estate, owned by the future Lord Aberdare. Socially and geographically it was a vantage point from which to witness the start of the most violent disturbances in modern Welsh history.

The south Wales farmers were up in arms. Prices had crashed just as cash demands on them soared. Already the new 1834 poor law was hated for cutting relief and raising rates. The rent charge was just as loathsome. Calculated from national prices, not depressed local ones, it raised tithes in the region by 7 per cent on average and up to 50 per cent in places. Payment was due promptly, twice a year and in cash. Peasants on remote farms lacked cash; their payments had always been flexible and in kind. The rent charge was intolerable.

Late in 1842 the farmers turned to violence. Toll-gates were targeted first, symbols of another hated tax. The rustics swooped at night, breaking and burning; vigilantes in drag, calling themselves 'Becca after their biblical 'sister' Rebecca, whose 'seed' was to 'possess the gate of those which hate them' (Genesis 24:60). In the spring full-scale riots broke out across the south-western counties, in Glamorgan, Cardigan, and Carmarthen. A thousand Rebeccaites stormed the Carmarthen workhouse; troops were sent in and scores arrested. Armed mobs roamed the countryside, avenging every injustice, threatening landlords, tithe owners, and their agents. By the autumn of 1843 attacks on persons and property were running at ten per week. A Celtic conspiracy was suspected. The gentry linked the riots with Irish nationalism.

In the chaos the tithe surveys were halted and Wallace found himself idle for weeks. He seized the opportunity and rambled into the hills, teaching himself botany and geology. In retrospect he saw this as 'the turning-point' of his life, the start of his scientific career (Wallace, 1905, vol.1, p.196). It was also the moment he became a political journalist, and ever after his science and politics were linked. One of his first compositions,

FIGURE 16/17.9 'Rebecca' in action as seen from revolutionary Paris. From an engraving by J.F. Dupressoir in L'Illustration, 1843, by courtesy of Mary Evans Picture Library

'The South-Wales Farmer', dates from the end of 1843. It failed to find a publisher, even though here Wallace shrewdly exploited his first-hand knowledge of the angry peasants.

EXERCISE

Wallace's essay, written when he was twenty, is his earliest known work. It strikes up themes that play for the rest of his life, some of which we'll explore later. So please turn now to *Resource Book 3*, B1, and read the entire essay, indexing its subjects as you go by placing letters in the margin: F = *food production* (human subsistence); E = *ethnic differences* (English–Welsh or Saxon–Celt); S = *supernatural beliefs* (religious and otherwise); P = *politics* (including socio-economic relationships).

DISCUSSION

You should have recorded many F's in the first part of the essay, as it deals with agriculture. In native Welsh country 'the system of farming is as poor as the land'. Custom reigns supreme, as in the stationary 'nations of the East'. Nor is there an incentive for improvement, for most farmers are tenants. When asked why he does not do thus-and-so, one will say 'he can't afford it' and demand to know 'where he is to get money to pay people for doing it'. Bare survival is hard enough, living 'almost entirely on vegetable food', never mind the 'turnpike grievances, poor-rates, and tithes'.

Such 'P' comments occur throughout the essay, often joined to E's. Wallace's sympathies are egalitarian and vaguely socialist. The Welsh hill farmer 'lives in a manner which the poorest English labourer would grumble at', yet he is 'hospitable even to the Saxon', his 'fire, jug of milk, and bread and cheese being always at your service'. He works hard and 'bears misfortune and injury long before he complains'. But the 'Rebecca disturbances ... show that he may be roused', and Wallace clearly sympathizes with the cause.

Most of your S's appear adjacent to the last part of the essay. We'll return to this subject when considering Wallace's spiritualism, but for now I hope you noticed how critical, even cynical, his remarks about religion are. By 1843 he had renounced his family's Anglicanism and become an outright free-thinker.

About the time Wallace wrote the essay he left his Celtic neighbours to teach maths and technical drawing in Leicester. He remained there for a year, continuing his own education in the town library. One day he picked up a notorious political tract, *An Essay on the Principle of Population* by the Rev. Thomas Malthus. First published in 1798, it had gone through many editions; the message in the later ones was as simple

FIGURE 16/17.10 'A Celtic groupe; such may be seen at any time in Marylebone, London', according to the radical anatomist Robert Knox in 1850, playing on prejudices against which Wallace defended the Welsh hill farmers. 'I merely state the facts, either quite obvious or borne out by history. War is the game for which the Celt is made. Herein is the forte of his physical and moral character: in stature and weight, as a race, inferior to the Saxon ... In the ordinary affairs of life, they despise order, economy, cleanliness; of to-morrow they take no thought; regular labour ... they hold in absolute horror and contempt. Irascible, warm-hearted, full of deep sympathies, dreamers on the past, uncertain, treacherous, gallant and brave. They are not more courageous than other races, but they are more warlike ... It is fortunate for mankind that the Celtic race is ... broken up into fragments'. From R. Knox, The Races of Man, 2nd edn, 1862, London, Renshaw, p.52 (quotation on pp.319-22). Reproduced by permission of the British Library Board

as it was grim. Humans always tend to reproduce faster than they can feed themselves. This is a law of nature. The excess population must be eliminated, and only three sorts of 'check' are possible: *'misery'* (famine, disease, accidents, war), *'vice'* (contraception, abortion, infanticide), and *'restraint'* from sexual intercourse. These three are inescapable; there is no alternative. Wallace, believing in human perfectibility, shunned all such pessimism, but his reading of Malthus was opportune.

Fresh from Wales and scenes of rural distress, he plunged straight into a harrowing catalogue of the 'checks to population in the less civilized parts of the world'. Native Americans, Nordic shepherds, Asian nomads, African hunters, South Sea islanders – humanity ancient and modern is passed in review, struggling and suffering, maiming and murdering, dying for want of food. Chapter after chapter evokes what Wallace himself had *just seen and experienced:* the paltry provisions, the filth and squalor, the rude agriculture, the ignorance, and the violence of the Welsh peasantry. Everywhere the superiority of English customs is assumed. The impact of Malthus on a young Englishman, now living in green and pleasant Leicestershire, was – as you'll see – unforgettable.

Wallace crossed into Wales again in 1845 and resumed surveying, this time on a large estate near Neath where he was also required to collect the rent charge. The tenants here were 'very poor'; some spoke no English and became confused, others 'positively refused to pay'. It was wretched work and made him 'more than ever disposed to give it all up if I could but get anything else to do' (1905, vol.1, p.245).

Evolution and the Amazon

Natural history beckoned. In spare hours Wallace had attended the 'Mechanics Institutes' at Kington and Neath, where free libraries and lectures offered scientific instruction to the 'labouring classes'. He even gave a few elementary science lectures himself and in 1847 actually designed and built the Neath institute's new home. His knowledge of nature was growing (recall his essay's lists of plants and soils), so he decided to make a living from it. He swapped chain and transit for gun and net, keen to collect birds and insects rather than tithes. In 1848 he and a Leicester friend, Henry Bates, sailed for Brazil to scour the Amazon basin. They would pay their way by shipping back specimens for sale to rich collectors, keeping the duplicates for themselves.

FIGURE 16/17.11 The Mechanics Institute building (later the Free Library) in Church Place, Neath, erected in 1847 for about £600. Wallace, the architect and general contractor, was no cowboy: he boasted that 'the total cost did not exceed the sum named by more than £50'. From A.R. Wallace, My Life, 1905, London, Chapman and Hall, vol.1, facing p.246 (quotation on p.245)

EXERCISE

Wallace now saw science as his destiny, rather like Darwin did when he started round the world on HMS *Beagle*. So, skipping ahead, let's pause to compare their early views on the most sensitive subject they would ever address: human origins. Wallace was twenty-eight years old when in 1851 he first met native South Americans along an Amazon tributary, the River Uaupés. Darwin was almost twenty-four at the time of his first contact, in 1833, when the *Beagle* reached the southernmost part of the continent, Tierra del Fuego. Both left vivid descriptions, which are extracted in *Resource Book 3*, B2 and B3. Read them now, answering these questions:

1   Briefly, how does Wallace's account resemble his essay on the south Wales farmer?

2   How do Wallace's and Darwin's attitudes to native peoples differ? Are you comparing like with like?

3   Can you tell which one, Wallace or Darwin, was an evolutionist *at the time of his encounter*? Why? (Hint: look for 'unwitting testimony' and consider the texts' value as primary sources.)

DISCUSSION

1   The similarities are striking. Wallace again comments on habits and customs, giving precise details of physical appearance, dress, domestic life, and temperament. He is sensitive to differences between the sexes and to the Amazonians' social and educational prospects.

2   Both men were stunned (not least by the naked women) but here resemblance ends. Wallace admires his 'true denizens of the forest'; Darwin abhors his 'barbarians'. Wallace behaves as the guest of 'interesting people', Darwin like a punter at a freak show, hardly believing the exhibits are 'fellow-creatures'. Wallace fears that the 'good qualities of savage life' will be lost to the 'vices of civilization'; Darwin considers his 'savages' so low that civilizing them is impossible.

The contrast would be more telling if the two had met the same tribe. As it was, the Amazonians in their maloccas seemed more civilized than the Fuegian nomads 'coiled up' on the ground. And the different climates no doubt also affected Wallace's and Darwin's perceptions. Clearly, Darwin feels revulsion at the same personal features that charm and fascinate Wallace – hair, skin, adornments, language – but the acid test of their attitudes would be to reverse the encounters, with Darwin meeting Amazonians and Wallace Fuegians.

3   You probably identified Darwin as the evolutionist. His text seems unwittingly to bear this out, for it repeatedly compares the Fuegians with animals. The last sentence even refers to the hereditary effects of habit, by which 'Nature ... has fitted' them to their wretched environment. This reads almost like an anticipation of Darwin's famous 'survival of the fittest' (as natural selection was known from the 1860s). Wallace's text, by contrast, seems unwittingly at pains to elevate the Amazonians, without a hint about a bestial ancestry. It is not their environment but 'the refuse of Brazilian society' that threatens to degrade them.

But did you note the dates of publication? Both texts came out *years after* the events they describe, seven in Darwin's case, two in Wallace's. This was ample time for the authors' views on human origins to change, so all you can reliably judge from the texts *as primary sources* is whether one or the other was an evolutionist *at the time of going to press*. And again, Darwin looks like your man.

History is full of surprises. Darwin was indeed a closet evolutionist in 1838 when he finished his text, but it closely followed the diary he kept on the *Beagle*. There he first made the animal comparisons, *not* as an evolutionist, but as a sherry-sipping Anglo-Saxon, shocked by naked savages. Wallace, by contrast, was an evolutionist even *before* setting foot in South America. He had embraced an ape ancestry for humans while still in Wales, although evolution is absent in his account.

Evolution, remember, was considered not only a damnable heresy but also a dangerous pseudo-science (p.95). Wallace lived dangerously, Darwin didn't. Scientifically as well as socially, they came from different worlds.

Darwin, the second son of a wealthy doctor, had attended public school and graduated from Cambridge. He was headed for holy orders when the *Beagle* set sail and he spent most of the voyage dreaming of a country parsonage. His post as captain's companion had come via the Anglican old-boy network – the same suave gents who founded the British Association for the Advancement of Science. At the Cambridge annual meeting in 1833, where the word 'scientist' was coined, the reverend professors proudly displayed Darwin's first shipment of South American fossils. He was called 'Philosopher' aboard the *Beagle* but at home he had become the model young scientist.

Nor did Darwin disappoint. Professionally on the make, he picked his way through the minefield of plebian heresies. Phrenology, the belief in cranial bumps, was to him so much heady nonsense. Mesmerism was worse, its trances proof of 'a diseased tendency to deception ... in disordered females'. As for the nebular hypothesis and evolution, these he *did* accept once safely back in London, but with total discretion. He kept his speculations – 'mental rioting' – in pocket notebooks, telling no one, least of all his clerical patrons. Human thought, he jotted guiltily, is a 'secretion of [the] brain', even our love of God – 'oh you Materialist!' (Burkhardt *et al.*, 1985–96, vol.3, p.96, vol.4, p.40; Barrett *et al.*, 1987, p.291).

Darwin had much to lose, Wallace everything to gain. His openness to scientific novelty was typical of his age and class. At Leicester he learned to mesmerize from an itinerant lecturer and gave demonstrations before 'small audiences'. At Neath he attended lectures on phrenology and had his character 'delineated' by getting his head shaved and 'read'. He even tried out the weirdest new science, 'phreno-mesmerism'. By touching the head of a mesmerized subject at random he allegedly produced the very emotion associated with each inner phrenological organ – 'fear', 'wonder', 'veneration', and so on. Such experiments, he declared, 'convinced me, once for all, that the antecedently incredible may nevertheless be true; and, further, that the accusations of imposture by scientific men should have no weight whatever against the detailed observations and statements of other men, presumably as sane and sensible as their opponents, who had witnessed and tested the

166
Thought (or desires more properly) being hereditary.— it is difficult to imagine it anything but structure of brain hereditary, analogy points out to this. — love of the deity effect of organization. oh you materialist! — Read Barclay on organization!! Avitism in mental structure & disposition, & avitism in corporeal structure are facts full of meaning. — Why is thought being a secretion of brain, more wonderful than gravity a property of matter? It is our arrogance, it our admiration of ourselves. —

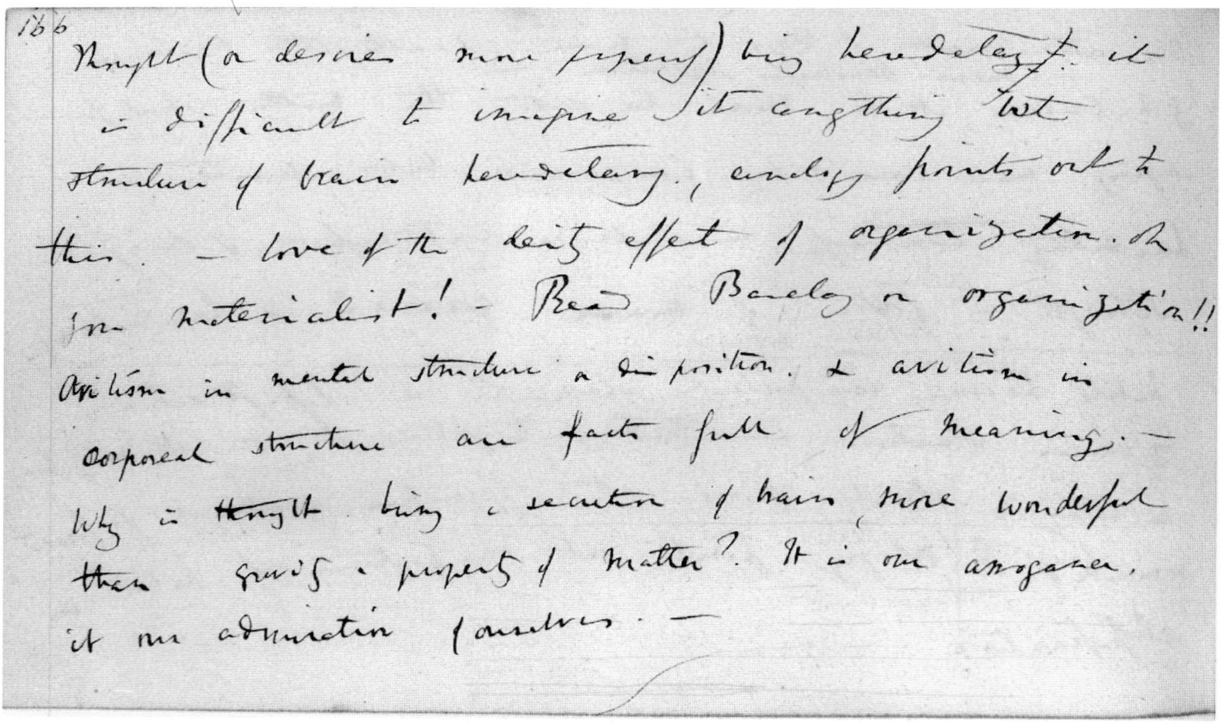

FIGURE 16/17.11 *Darwin's 'mental rioting' in a pocket notebook, mid-1838: 'love of the deity [is the] effect of organization. oh you Materialist! ... Why is thought, being a secretion of brain, more wonderful than gravity – a property of matter? It is our arrogance, it [is] our admiration of ourselves.–' From Darwin Archive 122, p.166, Cambridge University Library. Reproduced by permission of the Syndics of Cambridge University Library*

phenomena, as I had done myself' (Marchant, 1916, vol.1, p.24; Wallace, 1905, vol.1, pp.236, 257).

This was the voice of popular democracy and do-it-yourself research. Wallace believed himself to be no better or worse than a Welsh hill farmer, an Amazonian native, or a British Association bigwig. Thus he could live as an equal with 'savages' and sniff at élite savants. He was his own authority, without professional obligations, and so had no need, as Darwin did, to hide his belief in evolution.

It started at Neath in 1845 when he read the latest plebian potboiler, *Vestiges of the Natural History of Creation*. The book was anonymous, and no wonder: its sketch of material progress, from nebular gas up to human genius, was pure evolution – pure heresy. Rumours flew about the author and *Vestiges* sold like hotcakes. Some thought it was the offspring of a frail female mind – maybe wicked Byron's daughter? – and one of Darwin's reverend friends went over the top, calling it a 'filthy abortion' (Desmond, 1989, p.178). The real culprit was Robert Chambers, a publisher of popular periodicals, but no one knew for sure. Wallace didn't care. To him *Vestiges*'s vision of evolution was credible and one more science he would test: 'it ... furnishes both an incitement to the collection of facts & an object to which to apply them when collected'. He sailed for South America in 1848, not as Darwin had, to pursue an avocation, nor just to make a living, but to discover a 'theory of the origin of species' (McKinney, 1969, p.372; Bates, 1894, p.xx).

Four years passed. There was no rain forest eureka, no bolt from the Brazilian blue, even if Wallace did hint at 'some ... principle regulating the infinitely varied forms' of animals. His main achievement was to log the distribution of his specimens, labelling them carefully by locale. 'There must be some boundary which determines the range of each species', he decided; 'some external peculiarity to mark the line which each one does not pass' (1853, pp.83–4, 470).

FIGURE 16/17.13 *Wallace in 1848, age 25, on the eve of his Amazon adventure. From a daguerrotype reproduced in A.R. Wallace, My Life, 1905, London, Chapman and Hall, vol.1, facing p.264*

EXERCISE

Wallace had trained as a land surveyor. The business he knew best was drawing boundaries. Two of his maps appear in the *Illustration Book:* Plate 160 (a, b, c) shows the last map he made in Wales (of the parish where he was obliged to collect the rent charge), including an enlarged detail with Wallace's signature and a relevant schedule of fields; Plate 161 shows the map he drew of the Negro and Uaupés rivers in Brazil. Please study the maps *and* schedule carefully, noting at least three similarities.

DISCUSSION

One thing you surely found was that both maps are littered with labels: the Wales map has numbers for every field, the Brazil map names such as 'Macau indians', 'Manao indians', and (on the Uaupés enlargement) 'Tucanos' and 'Tarianas'. All these are in fact the names of tribes and refer, like the numbers on the Welsh map, to ownership or occupancy.

Another similarity is visible if you looked closely: a stream forms a natural boundary on the Welsh map, like the Brazilian rivers do. It marks the parish border on the south-east and from there meanders west. Some of the land farmed by 'occupiers' – tenants – like David Richards (fields 618, 619, and 669) is *bounded* on one side by the stream, just as the land occupied by, say, the Manao indians or the 'Gourmand Monkeys' (on the Uaupés enlargement) lies on one side of a river.

Although you may have detected other similarities, let me point out, finally, that the quality of the lands is also indicated for both maps: 'Alluvial Beds of Clays & Sands' where the Manao indians lived and the 'Brazil nut' grew; 'meadow' and 'pasture' (as per schedule) where David Richards fed his livestock.

Wallace's earliest fieldwork was on farms. Season after season he had lived among Celtic peasants scratching a living from rocky soil. He had surveyed their fields, collected rent charges, and observed their struggle for food. Darwin knew about such things, but as usual from the opposite side: by now he was himself an absentee landowner, living on the income from a lush Lincolnshire estate. He too saw hardship, but it was Wallace who understood it from below. To the Saxon surveyor and fledgling scientist, all nature was full of habitats where beasts and humans alike struggled to feed themselves and reproduce.

Mapping the Malay Archipelago

Undaunted by losing four years' collections on the return voyage from South America – his ship burned and sank at sea – Wallace sailed again in 1854 to capture wild life in the East Indies. There, according to *Vestiges*, he could also 'expect man to have originated', for the 'lowest' human races, 'the Malay' and 'the Negro', are found living beside the 'highest species' of apes (Chambers, 1844 &c., pp.296, 308). He made for the island of Borneo to find out for himself and at once engaged a teenage Malay boy to help him learn the language, teaching him in turn how to shoot, skin, and mount. Ali was an expert cook and boatman, and he remained Wallace's 'faithful companion ' throughout his travels in the archipelago (Wallace, 1905, vol.1, p.383).

They worked in Borneo for about a year, allowing Wallace to study all primates closely, orang-utans and native Dyaks alike.

> One wet day I produced a piece of string to show them how to play 'cat's cradle', and was quite astonished to find that they knew it much better than I did, and could make all sorts of new figures I had never seen. They were also very clever at tricks with string on their fingers, which seemed to be a favourite amusement.

And to think these people had 'only recently ceased to think head-taking a necessity of their existence'! Wallace did have 'a continual struggle to get enough to eat' because the Dyaks, in debt to Malay traders, would not sell him provisions. Even so, he marvelled, 'The more I see of uncivilised people, the better I think of human nature on the whole, and the essential differences between so-called civilised and savage man seem to disappear' (Marchant, 1916, vol.1, p.55; Wallace, 1905, vol.1, pp.343, 346, 350).

Other essential differences also vanished the more Wallace saw of orangs. He did take skins and skeletons – collecting was his job – but he also got to know one young ape very well.

FIGURE 16/17.14   *Wallace in 1853, age 30, about to leave for the Malay Archipelago. From the Wallace family archive. Reproduced by kind permission of John Wallace, Bournemouth, Dorset*

EXERCISE

Again, comparing Darwin and Wallace is apt. In 1838, after the *Beagle* returned, Darwin met his first ape – indeed, the first orang-utan ever to go on show at the London Zoo. Jenny was just a youngster and the keeper let him into her cell.

> The keeper showed her an apple, but would not give it her, whereupon she threw herself on her back, kicked & cried, precisely like a naughty child. – She then looked very sulky & after two or three fits of pashion [sic], the keeper said, 'Jenny if you will stop bawling & be a good girl, I will give you

the apple.['] – She certainly understood every word of this, &, though like a child, she had great work to stop whining, she at last succeeded, & then got the apple, with which she jumped into an arm chair & began eating it, with the most contented countenance imaginable.

(Burkhardt et al., 1985–96, vol.2, p.80)

Darwin was amazed by this human-like 'female' behaviour. Just compare it with a 'savage, roasting his parent, naked, artless, not improving yet improvable', he scribbled in a notebook, '& then let [man] dare to boast of his proud preeminence'! For good measure he added: 'not understanding language of Fuegian puts [them] on par with Monkeys' (Barrett *et al.*, 1987, p.79).

Now read Wallace's article, 'A New Kind of Baby,' in *Resource Book 3*, B4. It was first published in 1856 in a family magazine, *Chambers's Journal*.

1 How does the infant orang in this account differ from Darwin's Jenny?

2 Between the lines, what is Wallace's message?

3 The article appeared anonymously. What advantage do you think this was to Wallace?

FIGURE 16/17.15 *Darwin's Jenny, age 3, dressed for presentation to the Duchess of Cambridge. The youngster was bought by the zoo in November 1837 for £105; she died after an illness on 28 May 1839. Reproduced by permission of the Zoological Society of London Library, M. Lyster Collection*

FIGURE 16/17.16 *A female orang-utan like the mother Wallace shot, standing three and one-half feet high, with an arm span of over six feet. From A.R. Wallace,* The Malay Archipelago, *6th edn, 1877, London, Macmillan, p.41*

DISCUSSION

1   Both youngsters express 'feelings and passions' but Wallace's is conspicuously 'sweet-tempered'. It 'very seldom cries but when it wants to be cleaned or fed' and 'never screams and kicks' when bathed, 'as do many naughty children'. In short, Darwin's ape is a brat, Wallace's an angel.

2   Wallace is a wicked tease: the baby is really 'one of us' but he won't come out and say so. Instead, he appeals as a naive 'bachelor' directly to humanity's 'better-half', women. He answers every mother's questions about a new-born, then scouts her ready inference, 'the creature must be a monkey!' No, the little thing is tailless; it reminds him of the native 'Earthmen' children exhibited in London, or even the 'ape-like Aztecs'. Its colour is a 'mixture of all the races existing upon the earth', so it 'must be the descendant of some very primitive people'. Yet it must also have come of 'decent parents', for it has a respectable love of cleanliness.

   Sure enough, the baby is an ape. And 'I had killed the mother, so I determined, if possible, to save her offspring'. Was this homicide, then, or gallantry, or what? Wallace doesn't say.

3   Anonymity was an obvious advantage for a bachelor writing in a Victorian family magazine about killing a mother and failing to save her child. It also protected him from the damning aspersion that he believed humans had evolved from apes. Still, for all his coyness Wallace forced a shrewd dilemma on his prim, middle-class readers: the stronger their sentiment about his behaviour, the greater must be the presumption that apes are the moral equals of humans. This was, of course, impossible according to orthodox science: only 'man' has a soul. *Vestiges* had been slated for this bestial heresy; now here it was again, without a byline. No wonder Wallace sent his article to *Chambers's Journal*, published by the eponymous author of *Vestiges*!

Orang-utans intrigued Wallace. Their bodies mocked 'the "human form divine"' and, like Dyak tribesmen, they kept in one locale, their range marked by 'some boundary line' that they 'never pass'. He mused on the ape's ancient cousins, 'allied species still more gigantic ... and more or less human in their form and structure'. Did the Dyaks descend from these? (Wallace, 1905, vol.1, pp.343–5; Brooks, 1984, p.110).

In 1856 he sailed for the less explored eastern end of the archipelago but was delayed for two months on the small volcanic islands of Bali and Lombock. While collecting birds he noticed a remarkable change in fauna: 'The islands, ... though of nearly the same size, of the same soil, aspect, elevation and climate, and within sight of each other, yet differ considerably in their productions, and, in fact, belong to two quite distinct zoological provinces.' Not just single species, but large groups of species – 'genera, families, and whole orders' – were absent on one island or the other. Placental mammals, for instance, were found only on Bali's side, in the western 'Indo-Malayan' region; marsupials only in the 'Austro-Malayan' zone, stretching from Lombock eastward. Here then, in August 1856, he drew his most famous boundary, still known to scientists and geographers as 'Wallace's Line' (Brooks, 1984, p.138; Smith, 1991, p.233; Wallace, 1869, pp.590–91).

Months later he was again struck by nature's contrasting 'productions'. As his native boat approached the island of Ké, off the south coast of New Guinea, he watched in amazement as the dour Malay crew – ethnic Asians – was mobbed by a boat-load of indigenous Papuans: 'forty black, naked, mop-headed savages, ... intoxicated with joy and excitement'. Comparing the groups 'side by side', he realized 'in less than five minutes' that they 'belonged to two of the most distinct and strongly marked races' on earth. 'Had I been blind, I could have been certain that these islanders were not Malays.' In the space of a thousand miles, he

FIGURE 16/17.17 *Kanowit chief from Sarawak on the Malay island of Borneo. Photograph in Sir Hugh Low Collection. Reproduced from* The Living Races of Mankind, *1901, London, Hutchinson, p.76*

FIGURE 16/17.18 *Papuan chief of the Central Highlands, Papua New Guinea. Reproduced from* Illustrated London News, *17 November 1919, p.779*

had crossed into 'a new world, inhabited by a strange people' (Wallace, 1869, pp.415, 417). Where then was *its* boundary? And whence had the Papuans come?

His work instantly acquired fresh zest. The field journal he had begun at Bali now bulged with racial notes. 'The human inhabitants of these forests are not less interesting to me than the feathered tribes', he jotted in March 1857. With hummingbirds or humans, life's laws were all the same. Separate races came from separate places. All mixing was artificial. The differences between Malay and Papuan ran as deep as the mighty sea that split the archipelago. They were ancient, and their origin continued to puzzle Wallace on 'all the islands' he visited (Brooks, 1984, pp.137, 164, 168).

He pressed on, sorting the islanders into two, surveying all races alike, birds, beasts, and humans. His mental map now stretched over a million square miles:

> In this Archipelago there are two distinct faunas rigidly circumscribed ... yet there is nothing on the map or on the face of the islands to mark their limits. The boundary line often passes between islands closer than others in the same group. I believe the western part to be a separated portion of continental Asia, the eastern the fragmentary prolongation of a former Pacific continent.
>
> *(Marchant, 1916, vol.1, p.67)*

From where the Papuans had come. Wallace wrote this passage on the tiny island of Ternate (pronounced Ter-náh-te) in January 1858. He signed and sealed the letter, packed his bags, and made the three-hour crossing to its eastern neighbour, Gilolo.

EXERCISE

Wallace's map of the Malay Archipelago is in the *Illustration Book* (Plate 162). Study it carefully (disregarding the dark 'volcanic belts') and note the following features: (1) the Indo-Malayan and Austro-Malayan regions; (2) the '100 fathom line' in each region, bounding the central 'deep sea'; (3) the dashed line – 'Wallace's Line' – running between the islands of Bali and Lombock (9 degrees south, 115 degrees east).

Now find Ternate and Gilolo (see enlarged detail). They lie almost exactly in the centre of the map (1 degree north, 127 degrees east). What runs between them?

DISCUSSION

You easily spotted another dashed line, though whether it passes between the islands or just through Ternate isn't clear. This marks Wallace's 'division between Malayan & Polynesian races' (the latter having subsumed the Papuans in his work).

In February 1858 Wallace perched on Gilolo and peered through the summer haze towards Ternate. These islands, like Bali and Lombock, lay within sight of each other and had the same mountainous volcanic terrain. Yet they too were separated by a real but invisible boundary. Mentally he now drew this line, marking the division between Malays and Papuans.

Then suddenly he remembered that day in Leicester fourteen years before when, just back from the Welsh hills, he read Malthus's *Essay* on population!

Discovery

You have now reached the holy of holies: one of those famous moments in the history of science when a flash of inexplicable genius is supposed to light the path of truth. Wallace, a land surveyor and self-employed specimen collector, is about to discover the most important theory in modern biology, natural selection. He achieves this independently, twenty years after Darwin, and half-way round the globe. Doesn't this show that anyone, anytime, anywhere, with the right luck or brilliance, could have done it? What further explanation is needed?

Of course I've prepared you to look at the history of science differently. What we seek is a *natural* explanation, not the mental equivalent of a miracle. We need to show how the full *context* of Wallace's career prepared him for this moment.

Unfortunately, his own best recollections of the discovery date from around the turn of the century, almost fifty years on. By then the story had been well rehearsed and it bears signs of a fading memory. (For instance, Wallace places himself on Ternate instead of Gilolo.) Even so, we must listen to the primary sources.

EXERCISE

Wallace's fullest account is in *Resource Book 3*, B5. It includes a simple sketch of the theory of natural selection (although the term itself is not used). The text has been divided into six segments, A to F, for easy reference. Review the discussion of Malthus above (pp.113–14), then read the Wallace extract and answer these questions briefly:

1   Which part of Malthus's argument did Wallace remember? (B)

2   Why could Wallace apply the argument so readily to animals? (C, E)

3   How far does Wallace's answer to the question 'Why do some live and some die?' depend on adequate food? (C)

4   Judging from the extract alone, what do you think was the 'something' that brought Malthus to Wallace's mind? (A, B)

5   Do you think the notion of the 'fittest' surviving 'suddenly flashed' on Wallace? (D)

DISCUSSION

1   Wallace remembered the 'positive checks' that caused misery to 'savage races'. These were mainly involuntary afflictions (unlike those of 'vice' or 'restraint') and some arose from want of food.

2   You could have answered in several ways, but basically the reason why Wallace glided from an argument about humans to a wider argument about animal populations is that he was an evolutionist. To him humans *were* animals. A natural law like Malthus's 'principle of population' applied to one and all.

3   Food is crucial to all aspects of survival, as it is in Malthus's argument. There is no escape from the 'effects of disease', or 'enemies', or indeed 'famine' without adequate nourishment.

4   Wallace remembered Malthus while facing his own mortality. He was suffering from an 'intermittent' malarial fever when he asked himself the question 'Why do some live and some die?' Obviously the fever is what jogged his mind – *except he doesn't say so.* Never, in fact, would Wallace reveal why he thought of Malthus. He only mused (in another version), 'Somehow my thoughts turned' (McKinney, 1972, p.160).

5   The sudden flash reminds me of a snapshot, with Wallace striking a pose, flattering himself. In any case, 'race' improvement, or species change, by selective survival – *natural selection*, Darwin called it – lay only a short quick step from his previous remarks about the survival of superior individuals (C). It did not take a 'brilliant spasm of thought' but merely the right circumstances for Wallace suddenly to see all nature in a long familiar light (Huxley and Kettlewell, 1961, p.74).

What were these circumstances? Wallace remembered only that he was ill and on an island – the wrong island in fact – when he thought of Malthus. Everything else about his recollection is abstract or disembodied. There is no social, political, or even geographical richness to it, nothing remotely like his vivid descriptions of Welsh hill farmers, Amazonian indians, and orang-utans. It lacks cultural context.

But wait – there is one *superior* primary source. Just ten years after the event Wallace wrote up his eastern adventures in *The Malay Archipelago*, his most famous book. Not once in a thousand pages did he mention Malthus or natural selection, although by this time he was famous as Darwin's 'co-discoverer'. He did, however, give a detailed account of his arrival on Gilolo in February 1858 *and* his discovery of the Malay-Papuan boundary.

EXERCISE

An extract from this narrative, based on Wallace's contemporary field notebooks, is in *Resource Book 3*, B6. Read it now, marking its subjects as you did in the Welsh hill farmer essay: F = *food production;* E = *ethnic differences;* P = *politics* (including socio-economic relationships).

Now take the next step. Wallace said, 'Somehow my thoughts turned'. Given this rich new context, picture to yourself his experiences as a Saxon in Celtic Wales: his early childhood in Usk, on the Welsh borders; the surveying, the hill farms and the Rebecca riots. Then recall his sojourn in Leicester, where he read Malthus, and his continuing interest in racial boundaries and habitats.

What do you now think might have 'turned' Wallace's mind to Malthus and evolution?

DISCUSSION

" contextual --

It probably wasn't his malaria, which merits only the phrase 'owing to illness most of the time'. (Anyway, several previous attacks had not brought on the new evolutionary insight.) What's most striking about the passage is its picture of ethnic division and dominance, or simply colonialism (your Es and Ps).

Wallace lands on Gilolo with a Dutchman's two sons, in a Chinese boat crewed by Papuan slaves. Above the beach stands an old Portuguese fort, now the site of a Netherlands government garrison. In Dodinga, where Wallace settles, all the occupants are 'Ternate men', Malays mainly, from beyond the racial boundary. The 'true indigenes' are of Papuan extraction and quite distinct. It is they who crew Wallace's boat and labour for the local 'Chinese and Ternate traders'. It is they who live in the mountainous interior, beyond 'a little abrupt succession of hills and valleys', and bring 'rice and sago' for sale each day in the village (your Fs).

Does any of this seem familiar? It must have to Wallace. He notes the ethnic differences, the agriculture, the economic relations. He thinks of the dominant Ternate men and mentally draws a line between the islands. He falls ill. Life is fragile here. He wonders how the locals survive, provisioned from hill farms by primitives. He wonders how *they* survive, these less civilized tribes. The socialist in him thinks of the Celtic farmers; of himself, the Saxon surveyor; of the tithes, the poor rates, the riots. Wars, famine, disease – these cut life off, check it ... *just as Malthus said.* Only the fittest to forage remain.

Half the earth away, surrounded by natives on a remote volcanic island, Wallace remembered the boundaries he had drawn in another ethnic world, in another island kingdom. Gilolo reminded him of Wales, and Wales of reading Malthus in Leicester, fourteen years before.

Or so it may be argued, which is all one can ever say in history. Explanations of Wallace's discovery will be endlessly debated. He himself did not settle the matter, nor can we. Contextualist history of science shows, however, that natural explanations are possible, without recourse to mysterious flashes of insight. It sets out the cultural *pre*conditions for scientific knowledge. Whether these are also *sufficient* conditions must then be argued from historical evidence.

I've just worked through the evidence for one such argument. You need not accept my conclusions, but at least you should now have a better grasp of what historians of science today *do*. In the next section you'll be asked to develop your own contextual explanation for another critical event in Wallace's life.

5 WALLACE AS SPIRITUALIST

In 1862 Wallace returned to London, exhausted. Eight years in the Far East, travelling 14,000 miles, had left him in 'a very weak state of health', but now the sale of his collections – 125,660 specimens in all – produced a small but steady income, freeing him to rest and write up his discoveries (Wallace, 1905, vol.1, p.386). He composed fluently, in a logical limpid style, and his papers came out like clockwork – on hummingbirds and hornbills, butterflies and bees' cells, and not least, on the geography of the Malay Archipelago, with the first map showing 'Wallace's Line'.

Back on his feet, he made the rounds of scientific London. Mornings at the British Museum, afternoons at the Zoo, evenings at Linnean Society conversaziones – everywhere he picked up the best advice and the latest gossip. He heard about young men manoeuvring and new names rising. Science was being transformed.

New scientists, new science

The young guard called themselves 'men of science' or 'scientists', which was misleading. Unlike old Whewell (who coined the word) and his clerical cronies, they owed their status more to merit than rank or wealth. Overworked and underpaid, they had won their spurs the hard way; engineers and naval doctors, surveyors and civil servants who had fought for funds and clawed their way to power. Even now, in the 1860s, some were taking top scientific jobs in the capital, pushing out the old British Association fat cats, their *bêtes noires* (pp.91–3). The Oxbridge dons with their cushy chairs, the City gents and dusty dilettantes all had divided loyalties; their science was yoked with God or mammon. The new model scientists saw themselves as single-minded professionals, beholden to no one; a rising élite uniquely qualified to lead an emerging 'scientific culture' (Yeo, 1993, p.32).

Their science matched their social ambition. It too was comprehensive, taking in life, the universe – everything. The old scientists' world, split into material and spiritual parts, was destined for history's dustbin, the new men insisted. Nothing now was sacrosanct, nothing taboo. Spiritual specialists like the Anglican clergy were worse than useless. Far from adding to knowledge, they simply blocked it. Asked how the universe was formed or living species originated, they answered 'God'. Asked about the human mind and body, they dragged in the immortal soul. For such men all questions of origins and human nature lay shrouded in miracle and mystery, even despite the enormous gifts of science to material progress – steam traction, public sanitation, the electric telegraph and more.

Science delivers the goods; this was the new men's knock-down argument. All great life- and labour-saving advances of the century had come from knowledge of *natural law*. Further progress would be made only as scientists like themselves discovered law and order everywhere. The origins and ends of things; life, mind, and morals – all would be shown to result from *uniform material processes*. Miracles and mysteries were finished; the spiritual specialists had to go. Britain's coming culture would be not just scientific but wholly secular.

Radicals had mooted this for decades; now here were respectable chaps, Fellows of the Royal Society, sounding off in public, baiting bishops, and

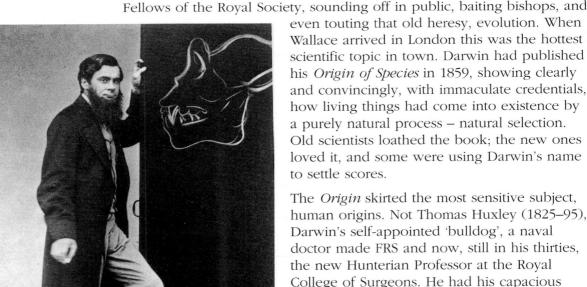

even touting that old heresy, evolution. When Wallace arrived in London this was the hottest scientific topic in town. Darwin had published his *Origin of Species* in 1859, showing clearly and convincingly, with immaculate credentials, how living things had come into existence by a purely natural process – natural selection. Old scientists loathed the book; the new ones loved it, and some were using Darwin's name to settle scores.

The *Origin* skirted the most sensitive subject, human origins. Not Thomas Huxley (1825–95), Darwin's self-appointed 'bulldog', a naval doctor made FRS and now, still in his thirties, the new Hunterian Professor at the Royal College of Surgeons. He had his capacious jaws clamped on the darling of the Oxbridge divines, Richard Owen, head of the natural history collections at the British Museum.

FIGURE 16/17.19 *Thomas Huxley lecturing on the gorilla about 1860. Photograph by Cundall, Downes and Company, London. Reproduced by permission of the Wellcome Institute Library, London*

Owen at sixty was a brilliant anatomist and fossil expert (he created the 'dinosaur' concept) with a fatal attraction for power. He was courtly, condescending, a Tory Anglican autocrat who hated evolution. His latest boast was that the brains of apes and humans are anatomically distinct; the latter could never have evolved from the former because the human brain had been 'especially adapted to become the seat and instrument of a rational and responsible soul' (Desmond, 1989, p.288). Huxley let out a snarl and set upon him. The tussle spilled into the press. He savaged Owen for shoddy methods and betraying science. The structural differences between humans and the gorilla were in fact 'not so great as those which separate the gorilla from the lower apes', Huxley growled. Humans had evolved in body and brain, and the only theory with 'any scientific' claim to explain it was the one 'propounded by Mr. Darwin' (Huxley, 1863 &c., pp.144, 147).

FIGURE 16/17.20 *Richard Owen, patrician palaeontologist: he had probably dissected more apes than any living person. Reproduced by permission of the National Portrait Gallery, London*

The origin of mind

Wallace was no stranger to this controversy. An old radical himself (though barely forty), he had read the bestial *Vestiges* and gone to Brazil in search of a theory of evolution. In the Far East he had lived with apes, comparing them with the locals, and hit on natural selection while pondering racial origins on Gilolo. He might have felt cheated when in 1858 the sketch of natural selection he sent to Darwin from Ternate was published without his permission, tacked on to extracts from Darwin's own work, establishing his priority. But no. Wallace, the self-taught specimen collector, was happy for the credit and honoured to have prodded the great Darwin into print. Overawed by the *Origin*, he even admitted, 'I really feel thankful that it has not been left to me to give the theory to the public' (Marchant, 1916, vol.1, p.73). Back in London the public made no mistake: the discoverers' names were linked. Wallace was counted a member of the scientific avant-garde and, like Huxley, a Darwinian defender of an ape ancestry for humans.

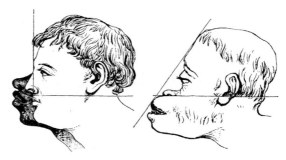

FIGURE 16/17.21   *'Profile of Negro, European, and Oran Outan', according to Robert Knox, whose ideas predominated in London's Anthropological Society. Racial superiority was thought to be directly proportioned to 'facial angle', making the 'grand classic face' the highest achievement of both nature and European art. From R. Knox,* The Races of Man, *2nd edn, 1862, London, Renshaw, p.404. Reproduced by permission of the British Library Board*

Not that the company Wallace kept was always respectable by Huxley's standards. He sought out radical allies in the new, men-only Anthropological Society of London. Its rooms were graced by a savage's skeleton and the meetings brought to order with a negro's-head mace. Here all subjects were debated with virile directness, and in an unseemly reaction to the prudery of the age the gents dwelt obsessively on such bare essentials as female 'circumcision', phallic symbolism, and the anatomy of the 'Hottentot Venus'. The main theme, though, was race, and the tone fiercely racist. (With the US Civil War raging, an agent from the pro-slavery southern Confederacy actually sat on the Society's council, channelling funds from the Richmond government.) Wallace did not share the extremists' views, but the 'Cannibal Club' (as members dubbed it) was the perfect place to stick his neck out. In a paper read before a meeting in March 1864 he became the first scientist in Britain publicly to apply the theory of natural selection to 'man'.

Rushing in where Darwin feared to tread, he tackled the fraught question of the origin of human races. Were they separate species, as the racists alleged, with the Caucasian the highest and the Negro next to apes? Or did all races descend from a single ancestor and share a common humanity (as Darwin himself believed)?

Wallace's answer was a clever compromise. He agreed with the extremists that the different *bodily* features of the human races – skin colour, hair texture, and so on – were developed from a homogeneous subhuman population in prehistoric times. These features had evolved by natural selection (or 'survival of the fittest') as adaptations to different environments, just like the skins and furs of animals. But once the races acquired human *mental* qualities, their bodily evolution ceased. When humans began to control their environment, building shelter, making weapons, raising food, and aiding one another, all further advance was due to the power of mind. Natural selection then affected not brawn but brain. The fittest to survive were no longer physically the strongest, but mentally the brightest and most moral.

EXERCISE

The closing paragraphs of Wallace's paper are in *Resource Book 3*, B7. Study the extract, marking the words and phrases that characterize humans as distinctive or unique. (*Don't* read the footnote to the final paragraph until you have answered questions 1 to 3.)

1   Older scientists and clergymen damned evolution for 'degrading' humans, making them mere beasts. What was Wallace's view? (Remind yourself of his attitude to native peoples and apes, pp.116–17 and 121–3.)

2   In what sense did Wallace believe humans were superior to nature? How far did he agree with 'Professor Owen' (p.131)?

3   Does Wallace explain the origin of 'that subtle force we term *mind*'? What do you think he meant by 'subtle force'? (Again, remind yourself about his early science, pp.115–19.)

Now read the final footnote. It gives the passage Wallace substituted in 1870 when he reprinted his paper in a book.

4   Comparing the passages, what new clue does he give about the origin of mind?

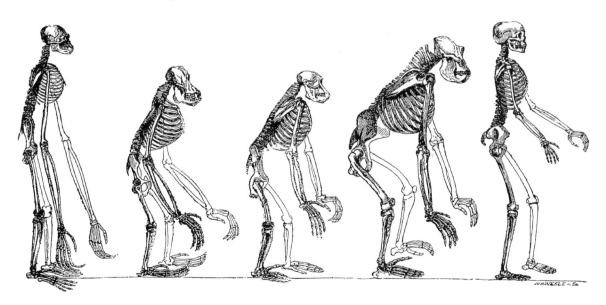

FIGURE 16/17.22   *Skeletonized 'man' tripping ahead of his grim relatives – gibbon, orang, chimpanzee, gorilla – as if queuing for an omnibus. From drawings by Benjamin Waterhouse Hawkins of specimens in the museum of the Royal College of Surgeons, London, reproduced in T.H. Huxley,* Evidence as to Man's Place in Nature, *1863, London, Williams and Norgate, frontispiece*

DISCUSSION

1   To Wallace evolution was *elevating*, not degrading. It had produced a supreme being, 'the head and culminating point of the grand series of organic nature', a being descended from and resembling apes but separated from them by an 'intellectual chasm'. On either side of the chasm, among orangs and so-called savages, Wallace glimpsed goodness and humanity (pp.116–17, 121–3). Evolution would go on perfecting humans until society and nature together became 'as bright a paradise as ever haunted the dreams of seer or poet'.

2   Wallace says that humans are 'in some degree a new and distinct order of being' and 'in some degree superior to nature'. The additional factor is their 'wonderful faculty' of 'mind'. By means of a 'superior intellect' and 'superior sympathetic and moral feelings' humans escaped the struggle for existence and entered a 'social state' in which they turned nature to advantage, preserving and enhancing life.

   This view agrees with Owen *only* in so far as Wallace (like a good phrenologist) identifies the advent of mind with the modification of 'head and brain'. Owen placed humans in a 'distinct sub-class', apart from other mammals, because he believed the human brain was anatomically unique. Wallace takes a similar line but does *not* follow Owen in ascribing the brain's uniqueness to its function as 'the seat and instrument of a rational and responsible soul'.

3   Wallace *nowhere* explains the origin of mind or why it appeared at once among the scattered human races. This is remarkable. Through mind, he declares, 'a grand revolution was effected in nature', yet the dawn of mind was itself surely a grander event, not least for having occurred (as stated here and elsewhere in the paper) at a particular 'moment'. But how the dawn came is unclear.

   The phrase 'subtle force' may stem from Wallace's early interest in mesmerism, the fringe science according to which one mind may control another at a distance (p.93). If Wallace meant mesmeric force, the great unanswered question is: How did humans acquire *this* power in the course of evolution?

4   I trust you immediately sensed Wallace's disillusionment. By 1870, eight years back in Britain, he realized that natural selection was *not* working as he had hoped. The 'fittest' (by his standards) weren't surviving; 'the mediocre ... both as regards morality and intelligence' were swamping them. To secure his utopian faith he seized on something old and something new: the 'glorious qualities' that, in his 1864 paper, distinguished humans from animals, and – the innovation – 'other and higher existences than ourselves, from whom these qualities may have been derived, and towards whom we may be ever

tending'. Not 'which' but 'whom': Wallace now sought the origin of mind among *supernatural beings*!

Darwin's co-discoverer was the cuckoo in the new scientists' nest. Between 1864 and 1870 he turned traitor to their programme of universal explanation by natural law. Indeed, his 'glorious qualities' and 'higher existences' were reminiscent of the immortal souls touted by the old scientists, the parsons, and Professor Owen. Just when their spiritual world was being banished, Wallace seemed to be letting it in through the back door.

 Why? Why did an accomplished naturalist suddenly break ranks and risk ridicule by embracing the supernatural? You may already have inklings of an answer, but do keep the question firmly in mind as you work through the next section. At the end you'll be asked for a considered response.

Conversion

Wallace's interest in spirits had been piqued years earlier. While still in the tropics he heard about the parlour craze sweeping Britain, the weird rappings and rocking tables, the 'miracles' and ghostly messages. He resolved to investigate when he got home.

EXERCISE

Look again at Wallace's early essay, 'The South Wales Farmer' (*Resource Book 3*, B1). You should have marked 'S' beside passages that mention supernatural or religious beliefs. Judging from these passages, what attitude do you think Wallace brought to the study of spirit phenomena?

DISCUSSION

He deplored 'superstition'. 'Wonders' performed by witches, the mystery of the 'corpse candle', 'dark omens of our future destiny', and 'supernatural agency' – all such beliefs are ascribed to ignorance, which only a sound education could cure.

At first Wallace *was* sceptical, and understandably. The spirit fad, or 'spiritualism', was the last wave in a tide of rural enthusiasms – revivalism, Mormonism, communitarianism, Adventism – that engulfed upstate New York in the early nineteenth century. The wave spilled over like all the rest and in the 1850s rolled into Britain behind a gypsy train of hucksters and hustlers known as 'mediums'. These adepts claimed to have contacts beyond the grave; for a fee they would prove it with a 'séance'. Parlours were darkened and hands held round a table. The spirits were invoked. Then the bumps would start, the table tilt, bells ring, breezes blow, candles burn, and objects would float in air. A message might be tapped out as if by telegraph or appear written on a slate. The showmanship was often spectacular, baffling unbelievers, who dismissed it all as fraud.

Yet many worthy persons were converted. Spiritualism satisfied the curious and soothed the bereaved (though some said they were self-deluded); equally it inspired radicals, who were keen to underwrite their political hopes. As a practical, empirical science, spiritualism served them even better than the old heresies, phrenology and mesmerism. Its appeal too was direct and democratic – all were potential mediums, anyone could join a séance – *plus* it guaranteed an upward social evolution. Spirit was seen as a progressive force, immune to earthly failure; the supernatural world would thus transform the natural, bringing in the millennium.

Spiritualism also held a special place for women. From the society matrons who launched the movement to the working girls who joined it in the 1870s, females of every age and class thrived in the charmed circle of the séance. As a domestic circle it was, of course, one in which Victorian women were thought to function best, yet the spirits seemed specially drawn to them and would perform avidly in their presence.

FIGURE 16/17.23 *'Table-moving' in its heyday: the whole family got involved. From* Illustrated Magazine of Art, *1853, by courtesy of the Mansell Collection/Time Inc., New York*

Shrewd ladies turned this to advantage, becoming prominent 'public mediums'. Impresarios like Mrs Mary Marshall and Mrs Agnes Guppy put on theatrical displays of power. Besides bringing messages from the dead, they were reputed to cause objects – even themselves – to levitate, materialize, or disappear. Under spirit control such women apparently held sway over the material world in a manner only dreamt of by male scientists and politicians. For this they were lionized, and radicals hailed the work of sister spiritualists as 'invaluable ... for the furtherance of meaningful social reform' (Owen, 1990, p.28).

FIGURE 16/17.24   *After the séance, 1870. Private collection. From R. Pearsall,* The Table Rappers, *1972, London, Michael Joseph, facing p.209*

EXERCISE

In what ways did the spiritual world of spiritualism differ from that of the old scientists and the Anglican clergy? (Look over pp.92–5 and 129–31 if necessary.)

DISCUSSION

The two realms were worlds apart. The old spiritual world was sacred and lay quite outside the old science. It could not be tampered with, for God and the soul were not experimental subjects. Also in this world, as in the material, a male élite officiated and policed the common boundary. There was no power-sharing with women. In spiritualism, by contrast, anyone could participate; the spirits could be beckoned and cajoled (God kept a low profile) and their antics manipulated. Females were spiritual specialists.

Wallace was drawn helplessly to spiritualism in the wake of his paper on racial origins. It was a turning-point in his life.

Single, shy, and over forty, Alfred was also tall – six feet plus – gangly and gauche. Never mind; he resolved to marry and was soon smitten with a woman of a superior class, still in her twenties. She resisted his attentions at first but he persevered, and in 1864 her father agreed to an engagement and a wedding date was fixed. Wallace himself takes up the story in a confessional letter to Darwin, written on 20 January 1865:

> For the last six months I have been doing absolutely nothing, & fear I shall not be inclined for work for some time to come. The reason is that I have suffered one of those severe disappointments few men have to endure. I was engaged to be married at Xmas, & had every reason to look forward to happiness, when at the last moment, when everything was arranged, & even the invitations sent out by the lady's father, all was suddenly broken off! No cause has been given me except mysterious statements of the *impossibility* of our being happy, although her *affection for me remains unchanged.* Of course I can only impute it to some delusion on her part as to the state of her health. You may imagine how this has upset me when I tell you that I never in my life before had met with a woman I could love, & in this case I firmly believe I was most truly loved in return.
>
> *(Darwin Archive 106/7 (ser. 2): 20–21, Cambridge University Library)*

Wallace never again saw or heard of the woman or her family. Nor would he ever experience 'such intensely painful emotion' (Wallace, 1905, vol.1, p.410).

Darwin's blunt advice – 'banish painful thoughts' through 'hard work' – was useless (Marchant, 1916, vol.1, p.160). Life had ground to a halt; serious work was impossible. As spring came Alfred crept on, trying to

FIGURE 16/17.25
Wallace at the time of his engagement in 1864.
From J. Marchant, Alfred Russel Wallace, *1916, London, Cassell, vol.1, facing p.142*

sort his insects, but he finally gave up. There was nothing for it but to up stakes and start over. Just before Easter 1865 he left lodgings in his sister's house and moved across London to live with his mother near the Regent's Park Zoo.

Three months later he began attending séances.

At first he sat with friends and picked up the usual tapping and vibrations. Then in the autumn he began visiting the matronly Mrs Marshall, who astonished him by making a table levitate and revealing details about his dead brother Herbert. Maybe an old mesmerist had such powers: Alfred practised at home for months without success. His sister, Mrs Fanny Sims, had an idea; she boasted that her new lodger, young Miss Agnes Nicholl, could produce 'curious phenomena' (Wallace, 1875, p.139). So in 1866 Alfred, Fanny, and friends began regular sittings with Miss Nicholl – later the famous Mrs Guppy. Now for the first time Alfred witnessed 'miracles' in his own parlour.

FIGURE 16/17.26   *Miss Agnes Nicholl in her late twenties, when she performed for Wallace: her considerable girth made the levitations all the more perplexing. Photograph by Henderson, by courtesy of Mary Evans Picture Library*

EXERCISE

Wallace's report of an early séance with Miss Nicholl is in *Resource Book 3*, B8. What techniques does he use to lend the report scientific credibility?

DISCUSSION

The report is detailed and matter of fact. Wallace anticipates objections – why Miss Nicholl stopped his turning up the gas, whether the room was secure – and asserts that the sitters (including presumably the medium) had no motive for deceiving one another. Among them were a doctor from Kilburn and a lawyer from Clifford's Inn, clearly reputable witnesses; names and addresses are given, all but inviting sceptics to make contact. The most telling element of scientificity is Wallace's description of the fresh-cut flowers and ferns which suddenly appeared on that December night. He gives both common names and technical – the orange-berried solanum, or nightshade; the Auricula Sinensis, or Chinese primrose – and he actually *counts* the stalks and blossoms. Here was the scientist at work, in the very presence of the supernatural!

Wallace was overwhelmed. Miss Nicholl soon showed him that she could raise herself, chair and all, 'instantaneously and noiselessly', to sit on a parlour table. She did so, he declared, 'some half dozen times, in different houses in London', before 'at least twenty persons, of the highest respectability'. (His account of one such séance is in *Resource Book 3*, B9.) This to Wallace was conclusive proof of spiritualism. He now knew not just 'the reality of the facts' but also their implication: they must be 'the manifestation of some strange and preterhuman power' (1867, p.255).

FIGURE 16/17.27
Wallace and a spirit manifestation produced by Mrs Guppy (née Nicholl) in a séance with the photographer F.A. Hudson, 14 March 1874. This was Wallace's 'first and only' visit to Hudson, a non-spiritualist. The 'male figure with a short sword' appeared during the second sitting (A.R. Wallace, Miracles and Modern Spiritualism, revised edn, 1896, London, Redway, p.196). Photograph in a scrapbook at the College of Psychic Studies, London

EXERCISE

You are now equipped to explain Wallace's conversion to spiritualism. This will not be simple, nor is there a single correct answer. Historians themselves have not cracked the problem (or even posed it well), so the most you can do is to suggest an answer, rather like I did for Wallace's discovery of natural selection. In both cases the same principles apply: the explanation must be both natural with respect to causes, and symmetrical with respect to what scientists call 'truth' and 'error'. These principles are set out on pp.99–102. Please make sure you understand them before going on.

1   Take the *naturalism* principle first. What sort of explanation does this rule out for *both* Wallace's discovery of natural selection and his conversion to spiritualism?

2   Now take the *symmetry* principle. This requires that both Wallace's discovery of 'truth' – natural selection – and his conversion to 'error' – spiritualism – should be explained in the *same* way, by reference to ordinary human processes. Having just ruled out one sort of explanation, list any other factors that might help account for Wallace's conversion. (Hint: look at this as a biographical problem, in the same way I posed the problem of natural selection's discovery on p.126.)

3   Take the final step: weigh up the factors you just listed and jot down your own *contextual* explanation (pp.104–5, 110) of Wallace's conversion. (I'll offer mine for comparison.)

DISCUSSION

1   The principle of naturalism rules out any explanation involving a non-natural or non-human cause. This means that Wallace's discovery of natural selection is not to be explained by the impact of nature itself or by an unfathomable flash of genius. Nor is his conversion to spiritualism to be explained by the action of *super*natural agents.

2   Your list may differ from mine but it could include the 'spiritual' phenomena (tables rising, flowers appearing, rapping sounds etc.), the broken engagement, Wallace's utopianism, the problem of the origin of mind, and his belief in mesmerism.

3   The conversion, as I see it, was a logical development of Wallace's long-term radical interests. He had been a phrenologist, a mesmerist, and an evolutionist for over twenty years. He believed that big brains in big skulls had enormous powers – unique powers, common to all humans without respect of race. Mesmerism showed him that the human mind was a 'subtle force', evolution that this force arose in a body descended from apes, and natural selection that this body

ceased evolving once it acquired a mind. The unanswered question in 1864 was, How?

Wallace made mind a *spiritual* entity added to the body, not evolved, only after witnessing Mrs Marshall and Miss Nicholl produce phenomena that he could ascribe to nothing but supernatural power. In 1866 this was, for him, a *scientific* solution to a *scientific* problem. He sought out these women, however, only after a severe emotional crisis, which adds another aspect to the story. Living with his mother, swayed by his sister, he remained vulnerable to forces – *social* forces – outside the male scientific establishment. No sooner had his fiancée misled him than he entrusted himself to female mediums, staking his scientific reputation on their integrity. In this paradox, perhaps, lies a deeper reason for Wallace's conversion, but fathoming it would require a full-scale biography.

FIGURE 16/17.28   *Wallace's deceased mother Mary Anne, manifested by Mrs Guppy on the third sitting with Hudson (see Figure 16/17.27). '[A]fter placing myself', Wallace explains, 'and after the prepared plate was in the camera, I asked that the figure would come close to me. The third plate exhibited a female figure standing close in front of me, so that the drapery covers the lower part of my body ... [T]he additional figure started out the moment the developing fluid was poured on, while my portrait did not become visible till, perhaps, twenty seconds later ... [T]he moment I got the proofs, the first glance showed me that the third plate contained an unmistakable portrait of my mother' (A.R. Wallace, Miracles and Modern Spiritualism, revised edn, 1896, London, Redway, p.197). From Georgiana Houghton, The Chronicles of the Photographs of Spirit Beings, 1882, London, Allen, pl.6, no.49. Reproduced by permission of the National Library of Scotland, K.203.D*

Parting with Darwin

Wallace had seen the light. 'The facts beat me', he insisted; 'if I have now changed my opinion, it is simply by the force of evidence' (1875, pp.vii, 132). Miss Nicholl's levitation had been crucial, and afterwards he threw down the gauntlet: 'Let those who believe it to be a trick, devote themselves to practise it, and when they are able to succeed in repeating the experiment, *under exactly the same conditions*, I will allow that some far more conclusive proof of the reality of these manifestations is required' (1867, p.255).

So the onus was on sceptics. Wallace made sure of it by writing a small pamphlet with a big title, *The Scientific Aspect of the Supernatural: Indicating the Desirableness of an Experimental Enquiry by Men of Science into the Alleged Powers of Clairvoyants and Mediums*. In late 1866 he rushed copies to the 'men of science' he respected most, including Darwin's pit-bull Thomas Huxley.

> Dear Huxley, – I have been writing a little on a *new branch* of Anthropology, and as I have taken your name in vain on the title-page I send you a copy. I fear you will be much shocked, but I can't help it; and before finally deciding that we are all mad I hope you will come and see some very curious phenomena which we can show you, *among friends only*. We meet every Friday evening, and hope you will come sometimes, as we wish for the fullest investigation, and shall be only too grateful to you or anyone else who will show us how and where we are deceived.

Huxley had had his fill of séances years before and hated the supernatural. He dissembled brilliantly, stating that he himself was too busy with *real* scientific research to indulge in female chit-chat.

> Dear Wallace, – I am neither shocked nor disposed to issue a Commission of Lunacy against you. It may be all true, for anything I know to the contrary, but really I cannot get up any interest in the subject. I never cared for gossip in my life, and disembodied gossip, such as these worthy ghosts supply their friends with, is not more interesting to me than any other. As for investigating the matter, I have half-a-dozen investigations of infinitely greater interest to me to which any spare time I may have will be devoted. I give it up for the same reason I abstain from chess – it's too amusing to be fair work, and too hard work to be amusing.

Wallace was not amused. He tried to raise the tone by invoking Michael Faraday, then the foremost experimental physicist (and since pictured on £20 notes), who had exposed 'table-turning' in the 1850s.

> Dear Huxley, – Thanks for your note. Of course, I have no wish to press on you an inquiry for which you have neither time nor inclination. As for the 'gossip' you speak of, I care for it as little as you can do, but what I do feel an intense interest in is the exhibition of *force* where force has been declared *impossible*, and of *intelligence* from a source the very mention of which has been deemed an *absurdity*.

Faraday has declared (apropos this subject) that he who can prove the existence or exertion of force, if but the lifting of a single ounce, by a power not yet recognised by science, will deserve and assuredly receive applause and gratitude ... I believe I can now show such a force, and I trust some of the physicists may be found to admit its importance and examine into it.

(Marchant, 1916, vol.2, pp.187–8)

EXERCISE

Wallace, a Darwinian scientist, disagreed categorically with Huxley, another Darwinian scientist, about the significance of spirit phenomena. Who then was being 'scientific' about the subject? Why? (Hint: this is a 'boundary' problem as discussed on p.103. Be sure to answer as a *historian of science* would.)

DISCUSSION

They *both* were being 'scientific', each according to his lights. The dispute was over where to draw the line between science and non-science. To Huxley being 'scientific' meant investigating natural subjects in suitable ways. Spiritualism was not a natural subject, so its phenomena had no place in *his* science. To Wallace being 'scientific' meant investigating all phenomena, even those deemed impossible or absurd. Spiritualism was proved by its phenomena, so they became integral to *his* science. This science included the supernatural; Huxley's denied it. Wallace saw himself as working on 'a *new branch* of Anthropology'; Huxley remained loyal to Darwin's. *Neither* branch, however, was seen as 'scientific' by the old scientists and the clergy, who not only kept spiritual things out of science but rejected evolution as well. The question for everyone in the 1860s was simply: Whose science will win?

By the time Wallace's pamphlet reached Darwin, they had struck up a lively correspondence. Socially and intellectually Wallace was the junior partner, but his transparent sincerity, encyclopaedic knowledge and persuasive powers impressed Darwin enormously – so much that in 1868 he confessed, 'I grieve to differ from you, and it actually terrifies me, and makes me constantly distrust myself' (Marchant, 1916, vol.1, p.227).

Conflicts were now emerging, mostly technical ones about the application of their theory. Wallace defended natural selection superbly, arguing only about how much it could explain. Darwin had admired his paper on racial evolution, but after receiving the spiritualist pamphlet he worried more and more. In 1869, on hearing that Wallace would review his old friend Charles Lyell's famous textbook, *Principles of Geology*, he despaired. Lyell had crushed him by refusing to 'go the whole orang' on human origins. Now Wallace threatened worse: to backslide. 'I hope',

Darwin shuddered, 'you have not murdered too completely your own and my child' (Marchant, 1916, vol.1, p.241).

His fears came true with a vengeance: the review was brutal. Its conclusion was so 'unscientific' that it seemed to Darwin to have been 'added by someone else' (Marchant, 1916, vol.1, p.243). Wallace now argued that neither the mind *nor* all bodily features of humans could have evolved by natural selection. Primitive people not only possessed mental capacities far in *excess* of their survival requirements; they also had physical features that were *useless* except in a civilized state. Their big brains, exquisite hands, naked skin, and speech organs had all evolved *prospectively*, long before they were needed, which showed intelligent foresight. Natural selection, being blind, could not have been the cause, so Wallace invoked a supernatural 'Power' to guide evolution.

EXERCISE

Darwin, feeling betrayed, stabbed exclamation marks and scrawled indignant notes beside Wallace's text. You can see this in Plate 163 in the *Illustration Book* (with the notes transcribed in the margins). Remind yourself about the two men's early encounters with primitive people (pp.116–17), then study the text and the notes, and state briefly what you think lay at the root of Darwin's objections.

DISCUSSION

The notes may suggest that Darwin was the more critical observer, but what clearly impresses him is the bare *suitability* of primitives' minds and bodies for survival, whereas Wallace was struck with their sheer *superiority* to the conditions in which they lived. Thus, Darwin's primitives had hands to 'tie knots' with; Wallace's Dyaks had hands for playing cat's cradle, and they taught him new tricks. At root, Wallace believed in the natural equality of 'savage' and 'civilized' peoples; Darwin didn't.

Reading Wallace, pen poised, Darwin suddenly realized how 'grievously' they differed and was 'very sorry for it' (Marchant, 1916, vol.1, p.243). Never again would he fully trust his colleague's scientific judgement.

Of course the review said nothing about spiritualism, and publicly Wallace had only called for an 'experimental enquiry', but Darwin still read blank credulity between his lines. It was all too much for him, even if Huxley could see one advantage: proving spiritualism true, he laughed, would cut the suicide rate. 'Better live a crossing sweeper than die and be made to talk twaddle by a "medium" hired at a guinea a *séance*' (Anon., 1871, p.230).

Vintage Huxley. More sober scientists, or those with less to lose, took up Wallace's challenge. The chemist William Crookes (who discovered the element thallium) constructed special apparatus and in 1870 began séances with the distinguished American medium Daniel Home. Darwin's true-blue cousin Francis Galton, a total sceptic, attended one and was 'utterly confounded'. In 'full gas-light', with 'perfect apparent openness', Home produced the most 'extraordinary' phenomena – even the playing of an accordion suspended by one hand! This was no 'vulgar legerdemain'; Crookes had taken 'thoroughly scientific' precautions. Galton begged Darwin to come and see for himself, but he refused, pleading ill-health.

FIGURE 16/17.29 *Charles Darwin about 1874. From a photograph by his son Leonard, reproduced in* Transactions of the Shropshire Archaeological and Natural History Society, *1884, vol.8, frontispiece*

Darwin only once sat in a séance, in 1874 at his brother's house in London. The novelist George Eliot was present as well as Galton and other relatives. The performance was about to start when Darwin broke the spell, made excuses, and went upstairs to lie down. When he returned he found the table stacked with chairs, which everyone said had been lifted over their heads, with sparks, and wind rushing, and strange rapping. 'The Lord have mercy on us all, if we have to believe in such rubbish', he groaned. His wife Emma, who had seen the show, explained, 'He *won't* believe it, he dislikes the thought of it so very much.' Smiling sweetly, she branded him a 'regular bigot'. Only after Huxley had attended another séance and declared the medium a cheat did Darwin relax. It would now take 'an enormous weight of evidence', he assured Emma, to convince him that there was anything in spiritualism but 'mere trickery' (Pearson, 1924, pp.63–7; Desmond and Moore, 1991, p.608).

The issues boiled up again at the 1876 meeting of the British Association. By now Huxley's new model scientists dominated the event, so there was uproar when Wallace, presiding over the anthropology department, allowed a paper on thought-transference to be read. The author was a physicist, William Barrett, who had worked under Faraday. The row splashed into the *Times* and got linked with the case of Henry Slade, a Yankee medium being sued by Huxley's protégé, the fiery zoologist Ray

So wallace had status that he lost?

FIGURE 16/17.30 *A séance in 1871: the theatrics had become spectacular. Private collection. From R. Pearsall,* The Table Rappers, *1972, London, Michael Joseph, facing p.64*

Lankester. Lankester had caught Slade cheating in a séance; Wallace had sat with him and seen only miracles. The case ended up in Bow Street magistrate's court, with Wallace as the star defence witness. Behind the scenes Darwin bankrolled the prosecution, which he considered a 'public benefit' (Milner, 1990, p.29). Slade was convicted and fled the country, his career as a con-artist in ruins. Wallace wiped the egg from his face and walked out of the British Association.

This was a defining moment. Spiritual phenomena were now ruled scientifically out of bounds. Barrett called on the British Association to appoint a committee to investigate spiritualism but no one listened. Nor was his thought-transference paper, a very 'model of caution', printed in the annual proceedings (Oppenheim, 1985, p.356). At the Association's 1878 meeting Huxley took Wallace's place as chair of the anthropology department and uttered a stern warning: 'if any one should travel outside the lines of scientific evidence, and endeavour either to support or oppose conclusions which are based upon distinctly scientific grounds, by considerations which are not in any way based upon scientific logic or scientific truth ... I, occupying the chair of the Section, should, most

FIGURE 16/17.31   *Prosecution of Slade the spirit medium, 1876. Prof. Lankester (giving evidence): 'You have already written on the slate; I have watched you doing it each time. You are a scoundrel and an imposter'. From* The Graphic, *14 October 1876, vol.14, p.361*

undoubtedly, feel myself called upon to call him to order, and to tell him that he was introducing topics with which we had no concern whatever' (Huxley, 1879, p.576). Wallace, who was absent, had got the message. He now met with a ginger group of intellectuals, who in 1882 joined Barrett, Crookes, and some fellow physicists to form an alternative scientific body, the Society for Psychical Research. It continues to this day, though its force was spent within a few decades.

EXERCISE

Earlier I explained that scientific consensus is formed by controversy, negotiation, and persuasion – pressures like those at work in ordinary politics (p.97). Review the present section and note down the pressures working in the 1860s and 1870s to *exclude* Wallace's spiritualism from the domain of science. (Hint: consider the relations among individuals and groups.)

DISCUSSION

The most important pressure came from the new model professional scientists, typified by Huxley, with their programme of universal explanation by natural law. Some physicists differed with the biologists, however, which may be ascribed to professional rivalry. Huxley's men saw spiritualism as a female fad, purveying 'gossip', so their pressure also derived from social forces affecting the relations of the sexes. Darwin himself differed with his wife about the subject and he ducked Galton's

invitation to visit Crookes. His authority was enormous. When he tackled Wallace about primitive people, his objections also cast doubt on Wallace's anthropological argument for a 'Power' behind evolution. Huxley's authority told heavily too, whether in slating mediums himself or priming others who did, such as Lankester. The British Association was a highly political forum (pp.91–3); by 1876 it had fallen largely under the new scientists' sway. Wallace's absence in later years, coupled with his disgracing in the Lankester–Darwin prosecution of Slade, is a conspicuous case of a scientist and his science being forced beyond the pale.

FIGURE 16/17.32 *Wallace in 1878, the professional pariah. From A.R. Wallace, My Life, 1905, London, Chapman and Hall, vol.2, facing p.98*

6 WALLACE'S SOCIALISM

Trespasser, traitor, or worse, Wallace does not wear labels lightly. He was awkward, independent, his young mind shaped by a plebian culture in which do-it-yourself science knew no bounds. In the 1860s, having travelled for a dozen years, he found himself back in London like Rip Van Winkle waking to a new world. He was famous now yet quaint and self-opinionated, a radical round peg among the neat square holes of the rising scientific professions. He never fitted in, never specialized, never unlearned. His science sprawled untidily, from phrenology and mesmerism, to Darwinism and spiritualism, to his last – and first – great interest, socialism.

Bad times

The 'great depression' returned him to his Owenite socialist roots (p.111). Between 1873 and the 1890s the first phase of industrialization ended in a flurry of banking crises, protectionism, and corporate restructuring. Britain, the last great bastion of free trade, paid dearly as exports crashed and unemployment soared: the 'workshop of the world' was being wrecked and its agriculture wasted. Cheap grain imports forced down prices just as a series of wet summers wiped out crops and drove farmers to the wall. Thousands left the land, exchanging run-down tenancies for rack-rented slums.

Wallace shared in the distress. He had married in 1866 (his bride Annie Mitten was just eighteen), but now with a growing family, and unable to find a full-time job, he left London and moved from place to place in search of an affordable home. His small investments (from the sale of his collections) dried up in the slump and he struggled to make ends meet, living from pen to mouth and marking school exams. Somehow he kept publishing first-rate research – *The Geographical Distribution of Animals* (1876), *Tropical Nature* (1878), *Island Life* (1880) – and it was for this, as well as his 'very striking' and 'original' discovery of natural selection, that Darwin himself came to the rescue. Winking at Wallace's spiritualism (which Huxley allowed was 'not worse than the prevailing superstitions of the country'), he used the full weight of his prestige to convince the prime minister, Gladstone, to grant him a civil list pension for distinguished service to science (Colp, 1992, pp.15, 17). In January 1881, as Darwin totted up his annual £8,000 investment income, Wallace marvelled at his own bonanza – £200.

That year he was elected president of the newly formed Land Nationalization Society. From his Welsh surveying days he knew the plight of tenant farmers; now with rural suffering rife, he saw private ownership of land as the root of all social ills. Nationalization was his panacea. By taking land into common ownership the State would

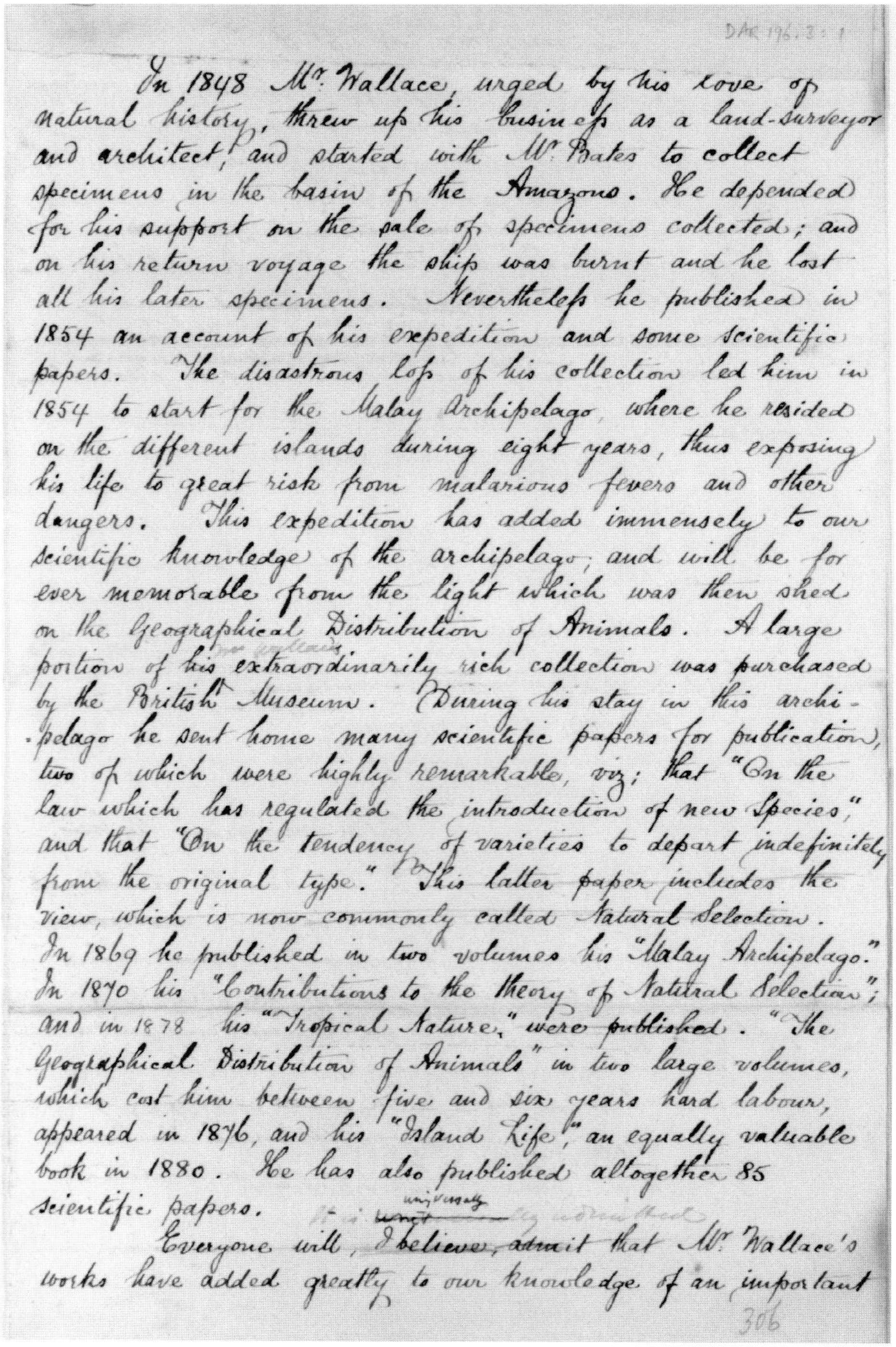

DAR 196.3: 1

In 1848 Mr. Wallace, urged by his love of natural history, threw up his business as a land-surveyor and architect, and started with Mr. Bates to collect specimens in the basin of the Amazons. He depended for his support on the sale of specimens collected; and on his return voyage the ship was burnt and he lost all his later specimens. Nevertheless he published in 1854 an account of his expedition and some scientific papers. The disastrous loss of his collection led him in 1854 to start for the Malay Archipelago, where he resided on the different islands during eight years, thus exposing his life to great risk from malarious fevers and other dangers. This expedition has added immensely to our scientific knowledge of the archipelago; and will be for ever memorable from the light which was then shed on the Geographical Distribution of Animals. A large portion of his extraordinarily rich collection was purchased by the British Museum. During his stay in this archi-pelago he sent home many scientific papers for publication, two of which were highly remarkable, viz; that "On the law which has regulated the introduction of new Species," and that "On the tendency of varieties to depart indefinitely from the original type." This latter paper includes the view, which is now commonly called Natural Selection. In 1869 he published in two volumes his "Malay Archipelago." In 1870 his "Contributions to the theory of Natural Selection"; and in 1878 his "Tropical Nature," were published. "The Geographical Distribution of Animals" in two large volumes, which cost him between five and six years hard labour, appeared in 1876, and his "Island Life," an equally valuable book in 1880. He has also published altogether 85 scientific papers.

Everyone will, I believe, admit that Mr. Wallace's works have added greatly to our knowledge of an important

306

FIGURE 16/17.33   *Extract from Darwin's memorial to Gladstone, December 1880, requesting a civil list pension for Wallace. Fair copy in Darwin Archive 196.3, Cambridge University Library. Reproduced by permission of the Syndics of Cambridge University Library* guarantee tenants the full fruits of their labour and ensure that all who wished to till the soil could obtain a modest plot. The countryside would thus be repopulated and the growth of cities checked. People would feed themselves rather than consume imported produce. Britain would prosper again.

Yet nationalization of land alone could not right the growing inequities of monopoly capitalism. Wallace glimpsed this in his 1885 Pears Soap prize essay about the depression, *Bad Times*, but he did not hit on a solution until four years later, when he read the most famous industrial utopia ever written, Edward Bellamy's *Looking Backwards, 2000–1887*. In this fictional forecast of life in the twenty-first century, capitalism has been transformed. The State is one great corporation, the sole employer and the final monopoly of the means of production and distribution. All share equally in its wealth, women and men alike. Wallace was overwhelmed by this vision, just as he had been by spirits. It seemed entirely 'realistic', and a second reading convinced him that Bellamy's logic was sound. He promptly declared himself a socialist (1905, vol.2, p.266).

FIGURE 16/17.34   *'Cheapside as a street of the type imagined by Mr. Bellamy': 'How complete the change had been I first realized now that I walked the streets. The few old landmarks which still remained only intensified this effect, for without them I might have imagined myself in a foreign town' (E. Bellamy,* Looking Backward, 2000–1887, *new edn, 1945, Cleveland, World, p.81). From Strand Magazine, 1903, vol.26, p.678, Bodleian Library, Oxford, Per2705.d.272*

Towards utopia: women's choice

A year later, in 1890, Wallace made the first 'scientific application' of his new creed in an essay that he later saw as his 'most important contribution' to 'the cause of human progress'. The essay's starting-point was the old problem of the survival of the unfit, on which he had heard Darwin comment 'very gloomily' (1905, vol.2, pp.209, 267; Wallace, 1890, p.325).

EXERCISE

Reread the last paragraph of Wallace's 1864 paper on racial origins *with* the passage he substituted in 1870 (*Resource Book 3*, B7).

1   How is the problem of the unfit solved here? How *well*?

2   How confident is Wallace about social progress?

DISCUSSION

1   Wallace simply invokes 'glorious qualities' and 'higher existences' – the supernatural – to solve the problem. He does not explain how, in *practice*, intellectual and moral 'advance' must come about.

2   The advance 'undoubtedly' occurs, notwithstanding the survival of the unfit, or 'low'; and Wallace is quite sure that it is 'on the whole a steady and a permanent' advance.

A few years later this would be whistling in the dark. The depression gave the severest shock yet to Victorian optimism and caused much practical soul-searching. If progress was not inevitable, pundits asked, what were its preconditions and how could they be achieved? To some (including most socialists) this was a purely political question; others saw a role for biology. Since social progress depends on the quality of individuals, they reasoned, and since individuals are the product of heredity, the first priority must be to improve the nation's 'stock'. Society can no longer afford to let its members reproduce at will, any more than farmers allow their cattle to. Selection is needed, the controlled choice of mates. The fittest must be *bred*.

Was there to be a State stud-book, then, with approved marriages and pedigreed babies? Some thought so; not Wallace. He dismissed all such schemes as illiberal or immoral. Humans were not bovine but naturally co-operative and sympathetic. Free them from tyranny, promote justice, and they would better the 'race' spontaneously. Social reform must come first; biological improvement would follow.

EXERCISE

Read the extract from Wallace's 1890 essay, 'Human Selection', in *Resource Book 3*, B10. It starts from the assumption that the social conditions described in Bellamy's industrial utopia have been achieved.

1   How is Wallace's scheme a *practical* advance on his 1870 solution to the problem of the unfit?

2   Twenty years on, what seems to be the missing element? Can you explain?

3   What weaknesses do you detect in the scheme?

DISCUSSION

1   The scheme is more practical to the extent that Wallace states what people must *do* to bring about 'race-improvement': first, reform society; then trust women to weed out genetic 'imperfections' by marrying well.

2   The spirits are missing, those old 'glorious qualities' and 'higher existences'. You might suppose that Wallace had given up spiritualism but in fact his belief was as strong as ever, quietly fuelling his optimism. Social reform would come about as people let themselves '*be guided* by reason, justice, and public spirit', race improvement as women manifest a 'still *higher* human characteristic', admiring the noble and shunning the base (emphasis added). Behind the scenes the spirits may still be glimpsed at work.

3   I hope you baulked at the notion that women are less passionate than men, or as Wallace assumes, that they tend to marry for security rather than sex. He reckons that when women achieve financial independence 'the number of the unmarried from choice would largely increase'. But why, if human nature may be changed, should women's sexual desire not improve? Why should the coming utopia remain, in this respect, quaintly Victorian?

    Wallace's assumption that fundamental social reform can take place *before* human nature improves is also problematic. How is utopia to be achieved without first eliminating 'the lower and more degraded types of man'? Or can the riff-raff be expected to co-operate in making a world that will wipe them out? For all its high-mindedness, Wallace's scheme reduces to the old muddle: 'We must first make the Utopian and utopia will follow' (Durant, 1979, p.51).

    The most serious weakness in Wallace's essay crops up often in his writings (you might recall *Resource Book 3*, B5) and is also present in Darwin's: the confusion of 'fittest' with 'best'. According to natural selection, the fittest organisms are merely those *biologically best adapted* to reproduce themselves. They *are* the survivors by definition, whether cockroaches or thugs. Wallace, however, assumed that the fittest humans must be *ethically the best*, so he rejigged evolution to *guarantee* their long-term survival: first, by making people progressive spiritual beings; second, by submitting them to 'human selection'. In both cases he found the key to the future in the hands of emancipated women.

Wallace's wishful thinking is only one example of the common Victorian conceit that nature is, after all, on the side of human hopes. But while many, including Darwin, made nature's slow, painful, Malthusian struggle the chief engine of social progress, Wallace saw progress guided by spirit. His 'fittest' and 'best' had transcendent qualities; Darwin's were only refined beasts. Evolution, accordingly, held alternative social outcomes, depending on its raw material. For Darwin the future lay in industrial capitalism, with its competitive, weak-to-the-wall ethos; for Wallace a socialist utopia was inevitable, where equality and co-operation would prevail. Both visions had fair claim to be called 'scientific' but they were based on radically different assumptions – assumptions that you've seen at work in Darwin's and Wallace's first encounters with apes, primitive people, and mediums.

Could it be that the joint discoverers of natural selection were actually never of one mind, even about 'their' theory? 'We shall, I *greatly* fear, never agree', Darwin once sighed to Wallace (Marchant, 1916, vol.1, p.209). Maybe he was right.

7 MR WONDERFUL

Today we apply the word 'wonderful' to things that delight us and people who please. It's a standard compliment. The Victorians had a subtler usage: they called something or someone wonderful just for astonishing them, for exciting interest or awe. *Wonderful Life*, Stephen Jay Gould's bestselling account of the half-billion year-old Burgess Shale fossils, enshrines this older meaning. To Gould the Burgess relics are 'wonderful' because they are extraordinary. He is intrigued by their peculiar structure, their amazing durability, and their power to illumine the past. In these units I've introduced you to Mr Wallace for similar reasons: because I too am intrigued by relics – his primary sources – intrigued by the man they reveal, his fads and foibles, his enduring reputation, and the light his career sheds on the history of science. Wallace's was a wonderful life as well.

This extraordinary man, who Darwin feared would 'turn renegade to natural history', was indeed a many-sided maverick (Marchant, 1916, vol.1, p.318). Geographer, evolutionist, and anthropologist, he was also spiritualist, socialist, and die-hard. His latter-day obsessions –

anti-vaccinationism (*pro*), flat earth theories (*con*), a finite universe (*pro*), life on Mars (*con*), and the verse of Edgar Allen Poe (he defended a hoax poem as authentic) – showed an obstinate disregard for professional propriety and earned him increasingly mixed reviews. Even allies became uneasy. Oliver Lodge, a fellow spiritualist and noted physicist, thought him 'a good observer ... with a great deal of self-confidence in the midst of much simplicity and modesty', but equally 'a crude, simple soul, easily influenced, open to every novelty and argument'. Amiable and honest, stubborn and naive, this was the wonderful Wallace, author of ten major scientific books, who, when proposed at last for a Fellowship of the Royal Society in 1893, at the age of seventy, could not see why he should be honoured: 'I really have done so little of what is usually considered scientific work', he demurred politely (Hill, 1932, p.34; Durant, 1979, p.33).

In 1898 his fourteenth book was published, *The Wonderful Century*. Most pundits that year crowed about progress; not Wallace. After sketching the century's successes, he dwelt forebodingly, chapter by chapter, on its failures: 'The Neglect of Phrenology', 'The Opposition to Hypnotism and Psychical Research', 'Vaccination a Delusion', 'Militarism', 'The Demon of Greed', 'The Plunder of the Earth'. Dotty and dismal, he pressed on until only his own inextinguishable hope lit the gloom. For despite the depletion of mineral resources, the clearance of primeval forests, and the extermination of native tribes; despite the 'hypocrisy and inhumanity' of the great powers, which had looked on coldly as a hundred thousand Armenians were massacred two years earlier – despite even this 'crowning proof of the utter rottenness of the boasted civilization of the Nineteenth Century', Wallace remained as certain as ever that 'true humanity' would prevail. Socialism was rising, with 'an unwavering faith in human nature' that had 'never been so strong'. The new century would see its triumph in a 'moral and social upheaval' equal to any of the past, one in which – he quoted William Morris – 'the bars of creed and speech and race, which sever, / Shall be fused in one humanity for ever' (Wallace, 1898, pp.377–9).

As in so much else, Wallace was proved wonderfully wrong. Mercifully, he died months before the outbreak of the First World War. Yet his own 'true humanity', his equal regard for 'the other', never failed. With Wallace's Line and natural selection, it forms his most enduring legacy.

In 1907 a young zoologist from Harvard University visited the island of Ternate, where fifty years before Wallace had posted the sketch of natural selection that pushed Darwin into writing the *Origin of Species*. Relishing this historic link, the zoologist set off for the hills with a party of locals, all draped with guns, nets, and bags. They were stopped on the road by a wizened old Malay man wearing a faded blue fez. He marched up to the Westerner in his collecting kit and announced proudly, 'I am Ali Wallace' (Camerini, 1996). And so he was: the same Ali who had been Wallace's 'head man' for seven years, who had cooked his meals, skippered his boat, and taught him Malay customs; the Ali who Wallace had trained as a collector and left a rich man in 1862, with money, guns, and supplies enough to set up on his own. Now in his dotage, Ali remembered *who* he was, and the man who had been his making: 'I am Ali Wallace'.

The zoologist snapped his photograph and posted it to England, where one bright morning, in his study overlooking Poole Harbour, Wallace tore open the parcel. Astonished and delighted, he sent heartfelt thanks. How well he too remembered his 'faithful companion', the young Malay who had stuck with him against all odds and even once nursed him through a malaria attack, saving his life. Theirs had been a human bond; they remained spiritual brothers. It was only right that Ali should share his name.

FIGURE 16/17.35
'My faithful Malay boy – Ali'. Wallace dressed him as a European for this photograph, taken at Singapore in 1862. From A.R. Wallace, My Life, 1905, London Chapman and Hall, vol.1, facing p.383

GLOSSARY

boundaries of science a map metaphor to aid understanding of internalist, externalist, and contextualist approaches to studying the history of science. The boundaries of science are established by scientists and philosophers to mark the limits of knowledge, institutions, and practices proper or 'internal' to science. What lies beyond or 'external' to these boundaries is called 'anti-science', 'pseudo-science', 'metaphysics', 'religion', 'ideology', 'irrationality', 'quackery', and so on. Scientists seek to defend the boundaries, though from time to time they may redraw them as the scope of science is changed.

contextualist history of science alternative to externalist and internalist approaches to studying the history of science. Contextualist history of science analyses the development of scientific knowledge, institutions, and practices by employing the full range of resources available in the humanities, regardless of whether these lie 'internal' or 'external' to any science as understood at a particular time. Contextualist history does not deny the existence of scientific boundaries; it only tries to understand how and why they have been established, without imposing boundaries of its own.

creationism in Jewish, Christian, and Islamic traditions, the doctrine that the universe was brought into existence by God, usually *ex nihilo* or out of nothing, and by processes unknown. In the nineteenth century most creationists also believed that God used miracles to bring the first individuals of all kinds of life into existence; thus they rejected evolution as God's method of creation. But many creationists have believed in evolution.

Darwinism after the English naturalist Charles Darwin (1809–1882); commonly thought to mean evolution and equated by scientists with Darwin's theory of natural selection; the doctrine that all kinds of life, including humans, were not created miraculously by God but have descended gradually from pre-existing organisms and ultimately from a few living entities or one, according to natural laws operating over a vast expanse of time.

evolution the doctrine that all kinds of life, usually including humans, originated by descent from pre-existing organisms or even nonliving matter. The physical universe, society, and many other things can be said to evolve by appropriate causes.

externalist history of science alternative to internalist and contextualist approaches to studying the history of science. Externalist history of science explains the development of scientific knowledge, institutions, and practices largely by 'external' - social, political, economic, and cultural - factors rather than by 'internal' factors based on reason and evidence. 'Externalist' was a shorthand used by internalist historians of science to denigrate their opponents (typically Marxist) but externalists themselves often wrote in a similar fashion to internalists because they assumed that factors explaining the development of science could lie 'external' or 'internal' to its assumed boundaries.

Golem Science science personified as the man-made creature of Jewish mythology, a powerful but dangerous being that does what it is told without understanding the 'truth' it pursues.

internalist history of science alternative to contextualist and externalist approaches to studying the history of science. Internalist history of science explains the development of scientific knowledge, institutions, and practices by 'internal' rather than 'external' factors. In this approach, internal factors are limited to reasoning based on factual evidence; they explain why science is cumulative and, on the whole, gives a better and better account of the world. External – social, political, economic, and cultural – factors lie beyond this rational boundary and account for deviations from scientific progress.

materialism commonly understood as a excessive attachment to material possessions; the belief that matter is the ultimate reality and that no entities exist independently of it, including God or gods, souls, spirits, and minds. People differ about what matter consists of.

mesmerism after the German physician Franz Anton Mesmer (1734–1815); a nineteenth-century fad, precursor to spiritualism and later called hypnotism; a set of informal beliefs and practices according to which one mind or brain may influence another, or its body, by means of an invisible force or fluid.

miracle commonly understood as a violation of the laws of nature; an extraordinary event attributed to a supernatural agency such as a god or spirit, apart from whose intervention the event would not have occurred.

natural selection the theory of evolution set out in Charles Darwin's *Origin of Species* (1859). According to natural selection, a struggle among ever-increasing numbers of individual organisms for the means of existence favours – 'selects' – individuals with any slight physical or behavioural advantage at leaving offspring in a given environment. The offspring tend to inherit the advantage; they struggle among themselves, are selected, leave offspring, and so on. Eventually, as environments change, offspring are born that appear so modified from the original parent stock that they can be called new species.

naturalism in science the assumption that all events can be explained by laws of nature and that all scientific knowledge properly so-called is of such laws and their effects. In the nineteenth century, scientific naturalism was predicated on three great generalizations: the atomic theory, the law of the conservation of energy, and evolution.

naturalism in the history of science the assumption that all scientific knowledge is a product of human activity and that neither nature nor any other non-human agency imposes it. What sustains trust in scientific knowledge, according to naturalism, is nothing more mysterious than human relationships.

nebular hypothesis a theory of the origins of the Solar System through the regular condensation of the planets out of the rotating nebulous atmosphere of the Sun according to the ordinary laws of physics and chemistry.

phrenology from the Greek *phrenos*, meaning mind; a nineteenth-century fad and would-be science according to which the 'faculties' of the brain that make up human character can be 'read' or measured from the external shape of the skull.

science from the Latin *scientia*, meaning knowledge; the practices, representations, instruments, and institutions by means of which knowledge of nature is produced. People differ about what 'knowledge' and 'nature' mean.

spiritualism an assortment of beliefs and practices based on the existence of disembodied personalities, including those of the deceased, who may perform miracles and communicate with living persons. Spiritualism does not require faith in God or Christianity but merely belief in an afterlife and a spiritual ultimate reality. It was a popular alternative to conventional religion in the nineteenth century.

supernaturalism a belief system in which beings – God or gods, souls, angels, demons, and the like – from an eternal, invisible, and intangible world may interfere with or manifest themselves in the ordinary course of events, causing miracles.

symmetry in the history of science a consequence of naturalism in the history of science; the principle that what comes to be seen as true in science is to be explained in the same way as what comes to be seen as false, by using the same kinds of historical causes or interpretations, rather than by appealing to some non-human agency.

two-track model a railway metaphor to illustrate internalist history of science. The two tracks correspond to the histories of scientific truth and scientific error, which in internalist history are explained in different ways, by appealing to different kinds of causes or interpretations, 'internal' and 'external' to science respectively. The model is peculiar to Units 16–17; like the football metaphor adopted to illustrate contextualist history of science (p.110), it is introduced to aid understanding.

REFERENCES

ANON. (1871) *Report on Spiritualism, of the Committee of the London Dialectical Society, together with the Evidence Oral and Written, and a Selection from the Correspondence*, London, Longmans.

BARRETT, P.H. *et al.* (eds) (1987) *Charles Darwin's Notebooks, 1836–1844: Geology, Transmutation of Species, Metaphysical Enquiries*, Cambridge, British Museum (Natural History)/Cambridge University Press.

BATES, H.W. (1894) *The Naturalist on the River Amazons: A Record of Adventures, Habits of Animals, Sketches of Brazilian and Indian Life, and Aspects of Nature under the Equator, during Eleven Years of Travel*, new edn, with a memoir by E. Clodd, London, John Murray.

BLOOR, D. (1988) 'Rationalism, Supernaturalism, and the Sociology of Knowledge', in I. Hronszk, M. Fehér and B. Dajka (eds), *Scientific Knowledge Socialized: Selected Proceedings of the 5th Joint International Conference on the History and Philosophy of Science Organized by the IUHPS, Veszprém, 1984*, Dordrecht, Kluwer, pp.59–74.

BLOOR, D. (1992, 2nd edn) *Knowledge and Social Imagery*, University of Chicago Press.

BROOKS, J.L. (1984) *Just before the 'Origin': Alfred Russel Wallace's Theory of Evolution*, New York, Columbia University Press.

BURKHARDT, F. *et al.* (eds) (1985–96) *The Correspondence of Charles Darwin*, 10 vols, Cambridge University Press.

CAMERINI, J.R. (1996) 'Wallace in the Field', *Osiris*, 2nd ser., vol.11, pp.44–65.

CARLYLE, T. (1838) *Sartor Resartus*, edited by A. MacMechan, Boston, Ginn, 1896.

CHAMBERS, R. (1844 &c.) *Vestiges of the Natural History of Creation and Other Evolutionary Writings*, edited by J.A. Secord, University of Chicago Press, 1994.

CLIFFORD, W.K. (1879) *Lectures and Essays*, edited by L. Stephen and F. Pollock, 2 vols, London, Macmillan.

COLLINS, H. (1992) *Changing Order: Replication and Induction in Scientific Practice*, new edn, University of Chicago Press.

COLLINS and PINCH, T. (1993) *The Golem: What Everyone Should Know about Science*, Cambridge University Press.

COLP, R., JR (1992) ' "I Will Gladly Do My Best": How Charles Darwin Obtained a Civil List Pension for Alfred Russel Wallace', *Isis*, vol.83, pp.3–26.

DEFRIES, A. (1928) *Pioneers of Science: Seven Pictures of Struggle and Victory*, London, Routledge.

DESMOND, A. (1989) *The Politics of Evolution: Morphology, Medicine, and Reform in Radical London*, University of Chicago Press.

DESMOND, A. and MOORE, J. (1991) *Darwin*, London, Michael Joseph.

DURANT, J.R. (1979) 'Scientific Naturalism and Social Reform in the Thought of Alfred Russel Wallace', *British Journal for the History of Science*, vol.12, pp.31–58.

GHISELIN, M. (1969) *The Triumph of the Darwinian Method*, Berkeley, University of California Press.

HARDIN, G. (1960) *Nature and Man's Fate*, London, Jonathan Cape.

HARDY, A. (1984) *Darwin and the Spirit of Man*, London, Collins.

HILL, J.A. (ed.) (1932) *Letters from Sir Oliver Lodge: Psychical, Religious, Scientific and Personal*, London, Cassell.

HUXLEY, J. and KETTLEWELL, H.B.D. (1961) *Charles Darwin and His World*, London, Thames & Hudson.

HUXLEY, T.H. (1863 &c.) *Man's Place in Nature and Other Anthropological Essays*, London, Macmillan, 1894.

HUXLEY, T.H. (1879) '[Address before the Department of Anthropology]', *Report of the Forty-Eighth Meeting of the British Association for the Advancement of Science; Held at Dublin in August 1878*, London, John Murray, pp.573–8.

KING, P. (1995) 'Historical Contextualism: The New Historicism?' *History of European Ideas*, vol.21, pp.209–33.

LAUDAN. L. (1977) *Progress and Its Problems: Towards a Theory of Scientific Growth*, London, Routledge.

MCKINNEY, H.L. (1969) 'Wallace's Earliest Observations on Evolution: 28 December 1845', *Isis*, vol.60, pp.370–73.

MCKINNEY, H.L. (1972) *Wallace and Natural Selection*, New Haven, Conn., Yale University Press.

MARCHANT, J. (1916) *Alfred Russel Wallace: Letters and Reminiscences*, 2 vols, London, Cassell.

MAYR, E. (1990) 'When is Historiography Whiggish?' *Journal of the History of Ideas*, vol.51, pp.301–9.

MILNER, R. (1990) 'Darwin for the Prosecution, Wallace for the Defense, Part I: How Two Great Naturalists Put the Supernatural on Trial', *North Country Naturalist*, vol.2, pp.19–35.

MOORE, J. (1997) 'Wallace's Malthusian Moment: The Common Context Revisited', in B. Lightman (ed.), *Victorian Science in Context*, University of Chicago Press, pp.290–311.

OPPENHEIM, J. (1985) *The Other World: Spiritualism and Psychical Research in England, 1850–1914*, Cambridge University Press.

OWEN, A. (1990) *The Darkened Room: Women, Power and Spiritualism in Late Victorian Britain*, Philadelphia, University of Pennsylvania Press.

PEARSON, K. (1924) *The Life, Letters and Labours of Francis Galton*, vol.2, *Researches of Middle Life*, Cambridge University Press.

RUSE, M. and WILSON, E.O. (1986) 'Moral Philosophy as Applied Science', *Philosophy*, vol.61, pp.173–92.

SMITH, C.H. (ed.) (1991) *Alfred Russel Wallace: An Anthology of His Shorter Writings*, Oxford University Press.

WALLACE, A.R. (1853) *A Narrative of Travels on the Amazon and Rio Negro, with an Account of the Native Tribes, and Observations on the Climate, Geology, and Natural History of the Amazon Valley*, London, Reeve.

WALLACE, A.R. (1867) 'Notes of a Seance with Miss Nicholl at the House of Mr. A. S–, 15th May', *Spiritual Magazine*, new series, vol.2, pp.254–5.

WALLACE, A.R. (1877, 6th edn) *The Malay Archipelago: The Land of the Orang-Utan and the Bird of Paradise; A Narrative of Travel, with Studies of Man and Nature*, London, Macmillan, first published 1869.

WALLACE, A.R. (1896, rev. edn) *Miracles and Modern Spiritualism*, London, George Redway, first published 1875.

WALLACE, A.R. (1890) 'Human Selection', *Fortnightly Review*, vol.48, pp.325–37.

WALLACE, A.R. (1898) *The Wonderful Century: Its Successes and Its Failures*, London, Sonnenschein.

WALLACE, A.R. (1905) *My Life: A Record of Events and Opinions*, 2 vols, London, Chapman & Hall.

WALLACE, A.R. (1913) *Social Environment and Moral Progress*, London, Cassell.

WHITE, M. and GRIBBIN, J. (1995) *Darwin: A Life in Science*, London, Simon & Schuster.

WILLIAMS-ELLIS, A. (1966) *Darwin's Moon: A Biography of Alfred Russel Wallace*, London, Blackie.

WOLPERT, L. (1992) *The Unnatural Nature of Science*, London, Faber & Faber.

YEO, R. (1993) *Defining Science: William Whewell, Natural Knowledge, and Public Debate in Early Victorian Britain*, Cambridge University Press.

READING WEEK

Apart from catching up on any outstanding work, the most useful thing you can do this week is get ahead with the literary texts for Block 5. Although the material on both plays (*Pygmalion* and *Medea*) will guide you through them from the beginning, it will very much help if you read the texts or listen to the performances on audio-cassettes 6–9. There is no substitute for knowing your texts in literary study – or music, so you could also listen to Richard Strauss's *Don Juan* on audio-cassette 11.

Unit 23 will begin with some very detailed work on the opening of *Wide Sargasso Sea*, so it will not depend in any way on your having read the text in advance. But of course you are free to do so if you wish.

If you have time, put your feet up with a video of *Jane Eyre*. It's not by any means necessary to know the novel to which *Wide Sargasso Sea* is a 'prequel' but you may be reassured to know the outline of the story. No film version is specially recommended; some may provide you with unintentional laughs. But a little light relief maybe just what you need at this point.

INDEX TO BLOCK 4

This index includes references to the Plates in the *Illustration Book*; these are indicated by 'Pl' for Plates.

AN INTRODUCTION TO THE HUMANITIES